AN OUTLINE OF THE RECENT HISTORY OF INDONESIAN CRIMINAL LAW

VERHANDELINGEN

VAN HET KONINKLIJK INSTITUUT VOOR
TAAL-, LAND- EN VOLKENKUNDE

DEEL XXXII

AN OUTLINE OF THE RECENT HISTORY OF INDONESIAN CRIMINAL LAW

BY

HAN BING SIONG

Springer-Science+Business Media, B.V. 1961

Additional material to this book can be downloaded from http://extras.springer.com

ISBN 978-94-017-4668-7 ISBN 978-94-017-4967-1 (eBook)
DOI 10.1007/978-94-017-4967-1

Aan mijn Moeder

ACKNOWLEDGMENTS

This essay was originally written for the Madjelis Ilmu Pengetahuan Indonesia as a contribution to its monograph series of "Penerbitan", but on the suggestion of the Council's executive director, Professor Soediman Kartohadiprodjo, it was decided to present the manuscript to a magazine abroad. The author is glad to find the Koninklijk Instituut voor Taal-, Land- en Volkenkunde willing to publish this study as a separate volume in its series of "Verhandelingen".

The author wishes to express his gratitude to Professor Soediman Kartohadiprodjo for his valuable suggestions, and to Professor G. J. Resink for his continuous encouragement.

Djakarta, April 26, 1960.

CONTENTS

INTRODUCTION

On September 29, 1958, nearly nine years after the transfer of sovereignty, the Indonesian legislature has at last endeavoured to end a rather peculiar situation in the criminal law, namely a state of territorial dualism in its codified part, in which it has all but succeeded. Before this date, there were two different criminal codes in Indonesia, one beside the other, each binding within its own territorial sphere of validity. These codes were the Wetboek van Strafrecht or Kitab Undang-undang Hukum Pidana, binding in Java, Madura and Sumatra except in the regions of Djakarta Raja and East Sumatra, and the Wetboek van Strafrecht voor Indonesië, valid for the two last mentioned regions and the rest of the Indonesian territory.[1]

From the names of the two codes mentioned above, an Indonesian and a Dutch one, it will be evident to the reader that this state of affairs was due to the fact that after World War II and before the transfer of sovereignty by the Dutch on December 27, 1949, there were two governments in Indonesia, the government of the Republic of Indonesia, proclaimed on August 17, 1945, and the Netherlands East Indies government, returned in Indonesia after the surrender of Japan. Each government enacted its own laws, and so, too, its own criminal law provisions, which in principle were only binding in the areas put under the effective control of each government. In short, with the presence of two governments in Indonesia, there were, side by side, two different legal orders in the country, each of which was maintained valid on December 27, 1949.[2]

The author will now try to give an outline of the most important developments in the criminal law of each legal order.

---

[1] Cf. M.D.B., Jrg. 3 1953. Territoriale verscheidenheid in het Indonesisch wetboekenstrafrecht, p. 29—32, J. J. Dormeier, *Pengantar Ilmu Hukum,* Part 2, 1955 p. 110, W. A. Engelbrecht and E. M. L. Engelbrecht, *Kitab*[2] *Undang*[2]*, Undang*[2] *dan Peraturan*[2] *serta Undang*[2] *Dasar Sementara Republik Indonesia,* 1956 p. 1472 and p. 1504.

[2] Cf. W. L. G. Lemaire, *Het Recht in Indonesië, Hukum Indonesia,* 2nd ed. 1955 p. 134.

CHAPTER I

DEVELOPMENTS IN THE CRIMINAL LAW OF THE REPUBLIC OF INDONESIA BEFORE THE TRANSFER OF SOVEREIGNTY

Basis of the new Indonesian legal order of August 17, 1945 was the decree No. 2 of President Soekarno of October 10, 1945 [3] which stipulated with retroactive effect that all regulations already in force on August 17, 1945 were to be maintained valid if not in conflict with the Constitution of the Republic and as long as they were not replaced by new provisions. So there was a continuation of the legal order of the Japanese occupant.

Unfortunately, complete information is only available about the laws and orders promulgated by the Japanese occupying forces in Java and Madura, not about the legal structure of the other islands.[4] This is probably due to the division of the Indonesian territory into three parts each under a different command: the islands of Java and Madura were put under control of the 16th Japanese Army with Djakarta as capital, while Sumatra was governed by the 25th Army with headquarters first in Singapore, later on in Bukit Tinggi, and the other islands by the Navy with headquarters in Makasar.[5]

February 28, 1942 [6] the Japanese forces landed on Java on three

---

[3] Peraturan Pemerintah 1945 No. 2, see Koesnodiprodjo, *Himpunan Undang², Peraturan², Penetapan² Pemerintah Republik Indonesia,* 1945 new ed. p. 34. Cf. Lemaire, *op. cit.* p. 249 and A. A. Schiller, *The Formation of Federal Indonesia,* 1955 p. 333. See also transitional stipulation art. II of the Constitution of 1945, Koesnodiprodjo, *op. cit.* p. 2ff.

[4] Cf. A. A. Zorab, *De Japanse Bezetting van Indonesië en haar volkenrechtelijke zijde,* diss. Leiden 1954, p. 9.

[5] Cf. Zorab, *op. cit.* p. 5—6, see also M. A. Aziz, *Japan's colonialism and Indonesia,* 1955, p. 160—161, F. C. Jones, *Japan's new order in East Asia 1937—1945,* 1954 p. 370—371, F. C. Jones, Hugh Borton and B. Pearn, *The Far East 1942—1946,* 1955 p. 74, G. McT. Kahin, ed. *Major Governments of Asia,* 1958 p. 494 and J. H. A. Logemann, *Het Staatsrecht van Indonesië,* 3rd ed. 1955 p. 30 who points out that there was a departmental organization in Java, while elsewhere there was only a regional organization. This is a possible cause for the fact stated above.

[6] Cf. Zorab, *op. cit.* p. 30. According to G. McT. Kahin, *Nationalism and Revolution in Indonesia,* 1952 p. 101 it was early on March 1, 1942.

places. March 2, lieutenant-general Hitoshi Imamura, commander in chief of the 16th Army, who came swimming to Bantam with a few staffofficers, issued a special decree consisting of ten articles.[7] Capital punishment and other severe penalties provided by Japanese martial law were to be imposed upon those who opposed the Japanese Army or were hostile to it, who were spies for the enemy of the Japanese, who destroyed oil installations, mines, estates and other sources, who destroyed the various sorts of communications such as roads, railways, telephone- and telegraphcables, postal communications, and who brought disaster to members of the Japanese Army, who burnt, plundered or destroyed military apparatus. Poisoning with the intention to bring disaster to the Japanese Army, entroubling the life of the people, destroying property, money and goods, and improper profiteering, as well as conduct contrary to the purposes of the Japanese Army or conduct that disregarded the commands of the commander in chief were also declared liable to punishment. Instigating to commit the crimes mentioned above or furnishing help could equally be punished with the same penalties.

At the same time the Gunsireikan (commander in chief) [8] promulgated martial law No. 1 [9] dealing with the penalties of martial law, referred to in the special decree. Principal penalties were capital punishment, imprisonment, exile and fine, while confiscation was an additional penalty. Capital punishment was to be executed by being shot, the minimum durance of the penalty of imprisonment was one month, and that of exile, which must be executed on another island, was one year, while the minimum of the fine was fixed to one rupiah. A fine could be inflicted together with the penalties of imprisonment and exile, and a substitute penalty of imprisonment for the durance of at least one day and at most five years should be fixed in case the convict could not pay the imposed fine. There was also a stipulation that a

---

7 Oendang-oendang (Nomor istimewa) dari Pembesar Balatentara Dai Nippon, in the official gazette *Kan Po,* Nomor istimewa, boelan 2 2603, p. 6. According to Oerip Kartodirdjo, 'De Rechtspraak op Java en Madoera tijdens de Japanse Bezetting, 1942—1945', T. 1947 p. 10, there were 9 articles.

8 As from September 1943 the title of Saikoo sikikan was used, cf. Logemann, *op. cit.* p. 31.

9 Osamu Gunrei No. 1 tentang hoekoeman menoeroet hoekoem Balatentara, *Kan Po* Nomor istimewa, boelan 2 2603, p. 4—5, see also Zorab, *op. cit.* p. 46—47.

convict might be dispensed from the execution of penalty in case the military commander considered it necessary. Beside these provisions concerning the penalties and their execution there were some other provisions. Art. 1 dealt with the sphere of validity of that martial law. It was binding for all inhabitants of the areas already occupied, only the Japanese themselves could not be punished by that law, unless no provisions were available in their own Japanese laws. Art. 2 stipulated that the following conduct should be punished according to martial law: rebellion against the Japanese army, spying for the enemy, endangering the security of the Japanese army, hampering military movements, and, — a really wide stipulation — every violation of the regulations of the Japanese commander. An attempt to commit those crimes could also be punished, and according to art. 3 even the preparations and the conspiracy to commit those crimes were punishable, as were the instigation of others to commit them and the help given to others who committed those crimes. Only if one confessed the crimes committed, might he be dispensed from those penalties, as well as in the case when he committed those crimes in such circumstances so that he should be pitied (art. 4). If one committed several crimes, several penalties could be imposed upon him, but he could also be punished with only one penalty, which was the severest (art. 12). These stipulations can be considered as general principles of criminal law, valid for all other criminal law provisions issued by the Japanese.[10]

By martial law No. 2[11] binding as from March 2, a court martial, named Gunritu Kaigi, was set up.

Djakarta was captured on March 5, and after Surabaja fell into the hands of the Japanese on March 7, decree No. 1[12] was issued by the Gunsireikan which contained an important rule of intertemporal

---

[10] Dr Zorab divides the rules of martial law No. 1 into general principles of criminal law and particular criminal law provisions, but according to the text there was not such a division. Only because of the very wide stipulation of art. 2 the rules concerning an attempt, preparation and conspiracy to commit the crimes mentioned in art. 2, and the rules concerning instigation and help, can indeed be considered as general principles of criminal law, not only binding at the application of the criminal law provisions of that particular law, but also binding at the application of all other criminal law regulations of the Japanese military government.

[11] Osamu Gunrei No. 2, *Kan Po* Nomor istimewa, b. 2 2603, p. 5.

[12] Oendang-oendang No. 1 dari Pembesar Balatentara Dai Nippon, *Kan Po* Nomor istimewa, b. 2 2603, p. 6—7. It may be assumed that in the other areas of Indonesia occupied by the Japanese there were similar rules of transitional law issued by the Japanese, cf. M.D.B. 'De gelding van vroeger recht in Indonesië', Jrg. 1, 1951 p. 8.

law in art. 3: all governmental institutions and their competences and all laws and regulations of the former government were recognized as still valid for the time being [13] as long as they did not conflict with the regulations of the Japanese military government. This meant an acceptance of the Netherlands Indies criminal law regulations, and thus a continuation of the validity of the Wetboek van Strafrecht voor Nederlandsch-Indië, the criminal code in force in the Netherlands Indies since January 1, 1918, except for the autochthonous population in certain regions in directly governed territory, which was left its own administration of justice,[14] and except for the subjects of the self-governing lands,[15] who were in principle subjected to adat law.

In art. 4 there was again a reference to the criminal law provisions of the special decree: anybody who disobeyed the orders of the Japanese army, or who endangered public safety, who hampered military movements, who disturbed or maltreated the Japanese, or who had contacts with the enemy, who brought disorder in the finances and economics, who held back goods, raw materials and products, should be punished severely according to martial law. Decree No. 1 was binding as from March 7, 1942.

Beside the various sorts of conduct penalized by the stipulations of the special decree, many other acts were declared liable to "severe penalties" (without any specification) by decree No. 2 of March 8,[16] which came in force on the date of publication.[17] For instance, associations and assemblies were forbidden, as well as listening to the enemy's broadcast.

In the beginning, trespassing all these orders and prohibitions had

---

[13] A provision contrary to international law, cf. Zorab, *op. cit.* p. 139, R. D. Kollewijn and R. van Dijk, *Staatsrecht en Rechterlijke Organisatie van Indonesië in overgangstijd,* stencil 2nd ed. 1950 p. 22.

[14] See, Ordonnantie of February 18, 1932 in S. 1932 No. 80. Only some stipulations of the W.v.S. N.I. were binding for these persons, see art. 3 *juncto* the appended lists B and C. See R. Supomo, *Sistim Hukum di Indonesia,* 3rd. ed. 1957, p. 55 ff and p. 96 ff. See also B. ter Haar Bzn., *Beginselen en Stelsel van het Adatrecht,* 4th ed. 1950 p. 12—13, or the translated edition, edited with an introduction by E. A. Hoebel and A. A. Schiller, *Adat Law in Indonesia,* 1948 p. 23 and p. 31. The translation is not entirely correct, see for instance M. M. Djojodiguno, 'Membaiki salah faham', in *Hukum* 1957 No. 1—2 p. 39.

[15] See Supomo, *op. cit.* p. 63 ff and 98 ff, Ter Haar, *op. cit.* p. 13—14, Ter Haar, Hoebel and Schiller, *op. cit.* p. 24 and p. 31.

[16] Oendang-oendang No. 2 dari Balatentara Dai Nippon, *Kan Po* Nomor istimewa, b. 2 2603, p. 7—9.

[17] According to Zorab, *op. cit.* p. 47, that date was March 10, 1942.

to be tried by the court-martial. But by decree No. 14 of April 29, 1942 [18] an organization of civil courts was set up beside the court-martial, which henceforth had to apply the special decree only.[19]

It is not the author's intention to give a full account of all Japanese laws and regulations, suffice it to mention only the first promulgated decrees which form the beginning of the legal structure during the Japanese occupation. Yet another decree of the Japanese occupant must be paid attention to, namely the Gunsei Keizirei,[20] the criminal code in force as from June 1, 1944 (art. 43 of that code), beside the Wetboek van Strafrecht voor Nederlandsch-Indië, to abbreviated as W.v.S. N. I., which was maintained valid.

Already when the Japanese commander in chief enacted his first decrees, a number of offences, punishable by the Netherlands Indies criminal law provisions, including the provisions of the W.v.S. N. I., were withdrawn from the scope of those regulations and submitted to the Japanese provisions.[21] For instance, destroying, disturbing or damaging electrical installations, telegraph- and telephonecables, destroying or damaging buildings, obstructing roads and waterways, endangering traffic on railways, capsizing vessels, disturbing postal communications, counterfeiting and speading rumours. When the Gunsei Keizirei came in force, some other provisions of the W.v.S. N.I. ceased to be operative, too.

Indeed, especially in the field of the criminal law — substantive as well as procedural — it will often be necessary for an occupying power to change the existing laws, since the protection given by the existing legal order to the interests of the occupant must in many cases be

---

[18] Oendang-oendang No. 14 tentang peratoeran Pengadilan Balatentara Dai Nippon, *Kan Po* Nomor istimewa, b. 2 2603, p. 13—14.

[19] Cf. 'Tjara mengoeroes perkara menoeroet Oendang-oendang No. 14', *Kan Po* Nomor istimewa, b. 2 2603, p. 15, see also Zorab, *op. cit.* p. 65—66. Literature about the judicial organization during the Japanese occupation: Oerip Kartodirdjo, 'De Rechtspraak op Java en Madoera tijdens de Japanse Bezetting, 1942—1945', T. 1947, Han Tiauw Hing, *Overzicht van de rechtspraak tijdens de Japanse bezetting,* Mededelingen van de Chinese Juristenkring 1948 No. 4 stencil, J. J. de Jongh, *Het nieuwe cassatie-instituut van Indonesië,* diss. Djakarta 1951, p. 55—57, Aziz, *op. cit.* p. 162 ff, F. R. Böhtlingk, *Staatsrecht in Indonesië 1942—1951,* stencil p. 18, Zorab, *op. cit.* p. 49 ff, E. Utrecht, *Pengantar dalam Hukum Indonesia,* 4th ed. 1957 p. 423—424.

[20] Osamu Seirei No. 25 2604, Oendang-oendang kriminil pemerintahan Balatentara, *Kan Po,* tahoen 3 No. 43 boelan 5 2604 p. 6—13.

[21] Oerip Kartodirdjo, *op. cit.* p. 11.

considered insufficient.[22] But according to international law an occupying power may change the existing legal order of the occupied territory only in so far as such a change is necessary for the security of its armed forces.[23] Many provisions of the W.v.S. N. I. made inoperative, however, concerned common crimes such as homicide, infliction of bodily harm, theft and rape. Therefore, according to Zorab,[24] the enactment of new provisions for those offences by the Japanese occupying forces was contrary to international law. It is not the purpose of this outline to evaluate the enactments of the Japanese 16th Army command. For that subject the reader is kindly referred to the dissertation of Zorab. But it must be conceded that there is no other conception more abused and more put forward as an excuse than the conception of military necessity, while on the other hand, the vagueness of that conception makes it almost impossible to apply a definite standard.[25]

The Gunsei Keizirei was divided into two parts, one containing general principles of criminal law, the other containing particular criminal law provisions which penalized various sorts of behaviour. The general principles were rules binding not only when the particular provisions of the second part of the Gunsei Keizirei were to be applied, but also at the application of all other criminal law provisions embodied in the regulations decreed by the Japanese occupying forces, unless when a special stipulation was provided (art. 2 of the Gunsei Keizirei). Before the issuance of the Gunsei Keizirei, the general principles of martial law [26] were binding at the application of those particular criminal law provisions. But, according to Zorab,[27] because these general principles were very brief and rather incomplete, in practice the general principles incorporated in the first book of the W.v.S. N. I. were applied by the Indonesian judges as a completion to the general principles of martial law whenever a decree of the Japanese containing a particular criminal law provision was to be applied. This practice

---

[22] Cf. J. P. A. François, *Grondlijnen van het Volkenrecht,* 1954, p. 765.

[23] Cf. Hans Kelsen, *Principles of International Law,* 2nd ed. 1956 p. 73. See also L. Oppenheim and H. Lauterpacht, *International Law,* II, 7th ed. 1955 p. 437 and p. 446, P. Guggenheim, *Lehrbuch des Völkerrechts,* II, 1951 p. 928 and p. 938.

[24] *Op. cit.* p. 146—147.

[25] Cf. M. W. Mouton, *Oorlogsmisdrijven en het Internationale Recht,* diss. Leiden 1947, p. 431.

[26] See note 10.

[27] *Op. cit.* p. 56 57.

was very unsatisfying to the Japanese. The general principles of the W.v.S. N. I. were only allowed to be used at the application of criminal law stipulations of the former Netherlands Indies government. In order to make an end of this practice the Japanese government issued the new penal code.

But perhaps it was not only the practice mentioned above that was the reason for the Japanese to make a criminal code of their own. To the author it seems to be the general intention of the Japanese military government gradually to set aside the Netherlands Indies laws as much as possible. Their policy was not only to prevent the application of the general principles of the Netherlands Indies criminal law to Japanese particular stipulations, but also to prevent the application of some particular criminal law provisions of the former legal order hitherto maintained binding. This policy, in the author's opinion, is also evident from the stipulation of decree No. 1.

The Gunsei Keizirei was binding for anybody who committed an offence within the territorial sphere of validity of that code, and also for persons who committed a crime outside that sphere in case they themselves were within it (art. 1). The Japanese themselves were not submitted to the stipulations of the Gunsei Keizirei, except when their own Japanese penal law regulations did not contain a provision.[28] According to the explanatory memorandum the territorial sphere of validity of the code was the territory of Java and Madura, including the strip of sea around it.[29] It was not explained what was exactly meant by the strip of sea around those islands. According to the text of art. 1, the general principles of the Gunsei Keizirei were also binding at the application of the Netherlands Indies particular criminal law provisions to persons fulfilling the stipulations of art. 1. But according to art. 2 the general principles of the Gunsei Keizirei had to be applied, not only to the particular provisions of the second part of the Gunsei Keizirei itself, but also to the offences for which punishments were provided by the other decrees and regulations of the Japanese military government, except in certain cases when there was a special stipulation in that particular regulation. The Netherlands Indies criminal law regulations were not at all mentioned. So, from art. 2 it can be concluded, in conformity with the explanatory memorandum, that the

---

[28] Cf. art. 3 Osamu Seirei No. 24 2604, Tentang mengadili rakjat Nippon, *Kan Po* tahoen 3 No. 43 boelan 5 2604 p. 5—6.

[29] Cf. Zorab, *op. cit.* p. 58.

general principles of the Gunsei Keizirei were not binding if any Netherlands Indies criminal law provision was to be applied.[30]

Art. 3 contained a rule about the temporal sphere of validity of the criminal law regulations of the Japanese military government: in case of an alteration of the law, the new regulation must be applied, but it was not allowed to impose a penalty more severe than the penalty provided by the former law. The text of art. 3 gives the impression as though it contained a rule only to be applied in the cases in which an already existing regulation has been changed. But it seems to the author that its stipulation contained a rule dealing with the temporal sphere of validity of the Japanese criminal law regulations in general, also to be applied in the cases in which a new regulation has been promulgated penalizing behaviour which previously was not liable to punishment, namely the rule that the regulations of the Japanese military government were binding with retroactive effect, or in other words, were binding unlimitedly, or absolutely.[31] In the Netherlands Indies criminal law the principle of non-retroactivity was binding: in art. 1(1) of the W.v.S. N.I. the principle of *nullum delictum nulla poena sine praevia lege poenali* was embodied.[32] Beside a rule of intertemporal law, there was a rule in art. 1 of the W.v.S. N. I. which stipulated that the criminal law must be statute law. In the system of the Gunsei Keizirei this rule was absent, there was no order that the criminal law must be statute law.

Only because of the exception in art. 3 could one not be punished for an act not yet penalized when committed, or be punished more severely for an act which, at the time of commission, was provided with a lenient penalty only. According to Netherlands Indies criminal law, the same was effected by the principal rule of non-retroactivity. For the Gunsei Keizirei itself, however, art. 47 stipulated that the code was also binding for acts committed before the code had come in force, except for acts not punishable at the time of commission. So, it was

---

30 See A. van Maanen, *Het Strafrecht van de Republiek,* T. 1947 p. 192 note 2, who has stated that the Gunsei Keizirei did not make any distinction between the validity of the general principles of the Gunsei Keizirei and those of the W.v.S. N.I. Only art. 1 was taken into consideration by Van Maanen, not art. 2.

31 Cf. P. F. A. Cremers, *Het Transitoire Strafrecht,* diss. Leiden 1884 p. 10.

32 See also art. 143 Indische Staatsregeling and art. 26 Algemeene Bepalingen van Wetgeving, *juncto* art. 2 of those Algemeene Bepalingen.

a stipulation based on the same principle of retroactivity, but more rigorous.[33]

If one committed a crime while at the time of the trial the penalty has already been abolished or replaced by a less severe penalty, he must be acquitted or sentenced less severely according to the principal rule of art. 3 of the Gunsei Keizirei. In the Netherlands Indies criminal law the same result was attained by the exceptional rule also embodied in art. 1 of the W.v.S. N. I., which stipulated that in case of a change in the law the most favourable stipulation must be applied. The only difference between the rule of intertemporal law of art. 3 of the Gunsei Keizirei and that of art. 1 of the W.v.S. N. I. is, that in case it is not possible to determine which of the two regulations is the most favourable one, the new regulation must be applied according to art. 3 of the Gunsei Keizirei, while according to art. 1 of the W.v.S. N. I. the old one must be used.[34] Contrary to the stipulation of the Gunsei Keizirei, in the criminal law of the Japanese home-land the principle of non-retroactivity is binding,[35] but the principle of absolute validity was included in the bill for a new Japanese penal code in conformity with the more modern views in Japanese jurisprudence.[36] So the Gunsei Keizirei at that time was more modern than the criminal code of the Japanese homeland itself.

Art. 4 of the Gunsei Keizirei dealt with the penalties and their order of gravity. Principal penalties were: 1. capital punishment, to be executed by being shot, except when that procedure was too difficult to be carried out (art. 5), a stipulation different from art. 11 of the W.v.S. N. I. which ordered capital punishment to be carried out by hanging. 2. imprisonment, which could be imposed for life or for the term of at least one day — which general minimum was not observed in the particular criminal law provisions of the Gunsei Keizirei itself, in contradiction to the provisions of the W.v.S. N. I., — and at most 15 years, which term could be extended to 20 years in case of augment-

---

[33] Compare no. 3 and no. 4 in the survey by L. Traeger, 'Die zeitliche Herrschaft des Strafgesetzes', *Vergleichende Darstellung des Deutschen und Ausländischen Strafrechts*, Allgemeiner Teil VI, 1908, p. 321.

[34] Traeger, *op. cit.* p. 321—322. See the sentence of the Raad van Justitie Medan, July 27, 1939, confirmed by the Hooggerechtshof, October 3, 1939, T. Vol. 150 p. 700.

[35] Cf. Traeger, *op. cit.* p. 325 and Kinsaku Saito, 'Das Japanische Strafrecht', in: *Das ausländische Strafrecht der Gegenwart*, edited by E. Mezger, A. Schönke and H. H. Jescheck, 1955 p. 224.

[36] Cf. Kinsaku Saito, *op. cit.* p. 326.

ation of the penalty, while for persons under the age of 20 there was a special stipulation (art. 6); and 3. fine, the minimum of which was fixed to one guilder. According to art. 30 of the W.v.S. N. I. that minimum was 25 cents. In case the convict could not pay the imposed fine, the subsidiary penalty was placement in a workhouse for at least one day and at most 5 years (art. 7). The maximum of the subsidiary penalty according to Netherlands Indies criminal law was 6 months, and in case of augmentation of the penalty 8 months (art. 30 W.v.S. N. I.). An additional penalty was confiscation, and art. 8 regulated what sorts of things could be confiscated. Different from the regulation of martial law No. 1, the penalty of exile was deleted. Art. 9 gave rules concerning detention of suspects without any limitation of duration, while art. 10—11 contained rules concerning suspension of the execution of punishment and concerning parole which were also different from the rules of the W.v.S. N. I. Very peculiar was the stipulation of art. 12: when a convict had to be released because he had served his time, he might be held in custody if there was some reason to expect that he would commit another crime again. Art. 13—17 concerned the instances in which there was failure to constitute a crime, and also about reduction and remission of punishment. According to art. 13, an act done in accordance with the law, or a justifiable act done in the course of due business or function, was not a crime, while art. 14 stipulated that an act done without criminal intent [37] did not constitute an offence,

[37] According to the explanatory memorandum, *dolus eventualis* was included, cf. Zorab, *op. cit.* p. 58. *Dolus eventualis* can be compared with that state of mind known in English criminal law as recklessness, ". . . . which has been judicially defined as 'an attitude of mental indifference to obvious risks' " and which ". . . . envisages the mind of a person who foresees the consequences of his conduct, and, though not seeking those consequences, deliberately takes the risk of their happening", thus J. Ll. J. Edwards, *Mens Rea in statutory offences,* 1955 p. 202, who describes that state of mind as an "I don't care" attitude. But it is pointed out by A. R. Tidow, *Der Schuldbegriff im englischen und nordamerikanischen Strafrecht,* Rechtsvergleichende Untersuchungen zur gesamten Strafrechtswissenschaft, neue Folge 5, 1952, p. 89, that recklessness also comprises "bewuszte Fahrlässigkeit", which according to Dutch and Indonesian jurisprudence must be distinguished from *dolus eventualis.* See Raad van Justitie Makassar, April 13, 1915 (T. Vol. 105 p. 208) which followed a way of thinking in conformity with the theory of Frank whose purpose it was to make a clear distinction between *dolus eventualis* and "bewuszte Fahrlässigkeit". It is a remarkable fact that *dolus eventualis* was already accepted explicitly by the Hooggerechtshof van Nederlandsch-Indië (the Supreme Court) in its decision of May 11, 1898, (T. Vol. 71 p. 15) while in Holland it was only accepted recently by the Hoge Raad der Nederlanden (*Nederlandse Jurisprudentie*

except when it must be punished, which is another peculiar stipulation. According to art. 15 an act committed by a person who is not able to distinguish good from evil was also not a crime at all, which was in accordance with the criminal law of the Japanese home-land.[38] Likewise an act committed by a person under the age of 12 did not constitute an offence. Different from the Gunsei Keizirei which used a psychological criterium: the ability to distinguish good from evil, art. 44 of the W.v.S. N. I. used a biological criterium: a pathological disturbance or defective development of the intellectual ability, combined with the requirement that the offender cannot be accounted for his act because of that biological defect or trouble.[39] It was not expressed by art. 44 of the W.v.S. N. I. that an act committed by a person meant by art. 44 does not constitute a crime, consequently Dutch and Indonesian jurisprudence very often makes a distinction between the liability to punishment of the act, and that of the person who commits the act. According to this opinion in the case of art. 44 W.v.S. N. I., the offender himself is not liable to punishment, but nevertheless his act is still a crime.[40] According to the W.v.S. N. I. an act committed by a person under the age of 12 did also constitute a crime, but for persons under the age of 16 special measures could be taken (art. 45 W.v.S. N. I.). According to art. 17 punishments might be

---

1955 No. 55, see also J. M. van Bemmelen, 'Erkent de Hoge Raad thans voorwaardelijk opzet?' *Nederlands Juristenblad* 1955 p. 69 ff.). Also in another respect the Hooggerechtshof was ahead of the Hoge Raad in Holland, see H. A. Idema, *De Indische Wetboeken van Strafrecht 1848—1934,* 1934 p. 458. So it is true that the judges in Holland could learn very much from the practice of the courts oversea, as it is pointed out by J. H. A. Logemann in his article 'Rechter en administratie overzee', *Rechtsgeleerd magazijn Themis* 1957 p. 81.

38 See Kinsaku Saito, *op. cit.* p. 241: "Verbrechen (Strafhandlung) ist schuldhafte Handlung, mit anderen Worten: Handlung, die auf Vorsatz oder Fahrlässigkeit des Schuldfähigen beruht; z.B. wird die Handlung einer Person, die das vierzehnte Lebensjahr noch nicht erreicht hat, oder einer Person, die geisteskrank ist, nicht Strafhandlung genannt".

39 Cf. H. B. Vos, *Leerboek van Nederlands Strafrecht,* 3rd ed. 1950 p. 90.

40 See for instance, D. Hazewinkel-Suringa, *Inleiding tot de studie van het Nederlandse Strafrecht,* 2nd ed. 1956 p. 132—133 and. p. 136; a different opinion is adhered to by W. F. C. van Hattum, *Hand- en Leerboek van het Nederlandse Strafrecht,* Vol. I 1953 p. 112, who does not make that distinction and who states that in the case of art. 44 no offence has been committed at all (p. 442). See also R. de Waard, 'De strafbaarheid van het feit naast de strafbaarheid van den dader', *Tijdschrift voor Strafrecht,* Vol. LIX 1950 p. 49 ff, Moeljatno, *Perbuatan pidana dan pertanggungan djawab dalam hukum pidana,* 1955, and Roeslan Saleh, 'Perbuatan pidana dan dipidananja pembuat', *Madjalah Hukum dan Masjarakat* 1958 No. 1 p. 3 ff.

reduced or remissed if a person who committed a crime turned himself over to the authorities. Art. 18 dealt with attempt, preparation and conspiracy to commit crimes, somewhat differing from the rules of martial law because the penalties could be reduced according to the circumstances, and also differing from the principles of the W.v.S. N. I. according to which preparations and conspiracy to commit an offence could not be punished except in some rare cases. Art. 19 gave rules for the following cases: if a single act was penalized by various criminal law provisions each providing a penalty for that act, second, if one committed various acts which were covered by the same criminal law provision, and third, if one committed various acts trespassing various regulations. For the first case the rule given by art. 19 was the same as the stipulation of art. 63(1) of the W.v.S. N. I., but for the other cases different stipulations were given. Art. 20 was about the cases in which two or more persons acted jointly in the commission of a crime, or in which one instigated another to commit an offence, or furnished help or assistance to the main offender. The penalties which might be imposed in the two first cases were the same as for a principal offender, whereas in the last case the penalty could be reduced. In the W.v.S. N. I. the rules binding for the two first cases were the same, but for the last case it was not possible to impose the same penalty as for the principal offender, which could be done according to art. 20 of the Gunsei Keizirei. Art. 21 gave an important decision about something that had been a question in Dutch criminal law, namely, one who collaborated with a person with a certain status or quality in committing a criminal act in which that status or quality is an element, could be punished as a partner even though lacking that status or quality himself.[41] If the weight of the punishment varied with one's status, a common punishment should be imposed upon the person who lacked that status. Art. 22—24 were stipulations about reduction of punishment according to the circumstances when the offender should be pitied,

---

[41] See G. A. van Hamel, *Inleiding tot de studie van het Nederlandsche Strafrecht,* 4th ed. rev. by J. V. van Dijck, 1927 p. 389 and p. 408, D. Simons, *Leerboek van het Nederlandsche Strafrecht,* Vol. I 6th ed. brought up to date by W. P. J. Pompe, 1937 (1940) p. 311 and p. 313, W. Zevenbergen, *Leerboek van het Nederlandsche Strafrecht,* 1924 p. 237 and p. 246, contra Vos, *op. cit.* p. 199 ff, Hazewinkel-Suringa, *op. cit.* p. 245 ff and p. 254, Van Hattum, *op. cit.* p. 378, 394 ff, 424 ff, W. P. J. Pompe, *Handboek van het Nederlandse Strafrecht,* 4th rev. ed. 1953 p.225 ff, T. J. Noyon, *Het Wetboek van Strafrecht,* Vol. I 6th ed. rev. by G. E. Langemeijer, 1954 p. 307 ff, 312 and 321 ff.

about how to reduce the punishments, and what to do if a punishment must be augmented and reduced on the same occasion. According to art. 25 imprisonment and fine could be combined, a general principle absent in the W.v.S. N. I.[42]

Another important general principle of the Gunsei Keizirei, absent in the W.v.S. N. I., could be found in art. 26, the last general principle of the Gunsei Keizirei. If a representative or an employee of a corporate body committed a crime which was connected with the activities of that corporate body, a penalty could also be imposed upon that corporate body. The penalty could only be a fine, and in case the fine was not paid, the activities of the corporate body should be stopped until the payment was done. These measures could also be taken against associations which are not corporate bodies. According to the Netherlands Indies criminal code, apart from the criminal law embodied in separate statutes, corporate bodies could not be the subject of any criminal act, a system also adhered to by the Gunsei Keizirei. But different from the Netherlands Indies general principles of criminal law (except the fiscal law) [43] the Gunsei Keizirei contained a stipulation which held corporate bodies and associations responsible for acts committed by its organs. Private persons could also be punished for crimes committed by their employees, beside the guilty employees themselves.

So, apart from the criminal law binding for the Japanese subjects which had exterritorial rights,[44] and apart from martial law, there were two systems of general principles of criminal law in Java and Madura, the general principles of the Gunsei Keizirei and those of the W.v.S. N. I. The determining factor was which of the particular criminal law provisions were to be applied, the Netherlands Indies regulations or the stipulations of the Japanese military government. Only some general principles of the Gunsei Keizirei were declared binding for the Netherlands Indies laws and ordinances. By art. 48 it was stipulated that the special provision concerning punishment of persons under the age of 20 (art. 6) was also valid at the application of laws and regulations of the former government to those persons, while according to art. 49 some provisions concerning parole (art. 11) and the provision concerning custody in case it was to be expected that the convict who had to be released for having served his term would commit another

---

[42] For an exception, see W. F. Prins, *Pengantar Ilmu Hukum Tata-Usaha Negara,* translated by R. Kosim Adisapoetra 1953, p. 23.

[43] See Prins, *op. cit.* p. 21 and note 166.

[44] Cf. Zorab, *op. cit.* p. 147, Aziz, *op. cit.* p. 163.

crime again (art. 12) were to be observed for persons sentenced according to the Netherlands Indies regulations. In case there was a concurrence of offences according to the Japanese criminal law regulations and of violations of the Netherlands Indies rules, the stipulations of art. 19 were binding (art. 46). This again meant a domination given to the Japanese general principle of art. 19 of the Gunsei Keizirei over the corresponding general principles of chapter VI of the first Book of the W.v.S. N. I. For the comparison of the penalties provided by the Japanese and Netherlands Indies regulations, a special table was also given.

By art. 27, 28, 29, 30, 31, 33, 34 and 35 penalties were provided for acts already penalized by the previous decree No. 2 of March 8, 1942, and also by the special decree of March 2, 1942. By art. 50 of the Gunsei Keizirei the respective stipulations of decree No. 2 were annulled.

According to the explanatory memorandum, all regulations of the former Netherlands Indies government which were in conflict with the provisions of the Gunsei Keizirei or any other decree of the Japanese military government were put out of effect automatically. Besides, it was not allowed to apply law provisions of the Netherlands Indies government which were not in accordance with the nature of the occupying military government, so for instance, the provisions of chapters I, II and III of the second Book of the W.v.S. N. I., and all ordinances of the Netherlands Indies military authorities.[45]

Art. 32 of the Gunsei Keizirei dealt with acts of violence and intimidation committed in association with others, a stipulation similar to art. 170 of the W.v.S. N. I., while art. 209, 210, 418,419 and 420 of that code were made inoperative by art. 36[46] which dealt with bribery: the public official who asked for or who received a bribe, and the person who gave it were punishable. Art. 37 was about homicide, and art. 38 about the infliction of bodily injury upon another person thereby causing his death. Carnal knowledge of a woman under the age of 15, or not yet grown up enough to have sexual intercourse with, and also carnal knowledge of a woman who had lost consciousness or who was unable to resist were provided with penalties by art. 39, so, too, carnal knowledge by force or by intimidation. By these provisions the art. 338, 339, 340, 341, 342, 343, 344, 351(3), 353(3), 354(2), 355(2), 285, 286, 287, and 291 of the W.v.S. N. I. were derogated and so annulled.[47]

[45] Cf. Zorab, *op. cit.* p. 61.
[46] Cf. Zorab, *op. cit.* p. 63.
[47] Cf. Zorab, *op. cit.* p. 62.

Art. 40 provided a penalty for the acts of robbing other people's property, taking unlawful advantage or letting other people have unlawful profit by using force or intimidation. Punishable as a robber was the thief who used force or intimidation in order to prevent the retaking of the stolen goods, to escape capture or to destroy evidence. Art. 41 and 42 gave the grounds to augment the penalties for robbery and theft: robbery and theft committed in association with others, committed against property of the Japanese army, committed during an air raid, or at night by forcing one's way into a house, a yard etc. So, some other provisions of the W.v.S. N. I. were also put aside, for instance art. 363, 365 and 368.[48]

Art. 44 altered the names of the penalties provided by the Japanese ordinances previous to the Gunsei Keizirei, while art. 45 did the same for the penalties already inflicted before the Gunsei Keizirei was put in force. Art. 50 and 52 gave specifications about what should be understood by the passage "should be punished severely" in decree No. 2 of March 8, 1942 and in decree No. 23 of July 15, 1942 concerning meetings and associations,[49] and what by the passage "should be punished severely according to martial law" in decree No. 21 of June 16, 1942 concerning the registration of radios and the restriction of the wave-lengths,[50] which indeed were indefinite formulations.

This in short was the Japanese criminal law, in principle maintained valid by the Republic of Indonesia on August 17, 1945.

However, many provisions were considered as contrary to the Constitution and to the status of Indonesia as a free and independent country, because many regulations of the Japanese were merely enacted in order to secure and to serve the Japanese military interests.

After the surrender of Japan, for instance, nobody obeyed any longer the restriction of listening to foreign radiobroadcast, since the prohibition was considered annulled automatically with the surrender of the Japanese forces. The regulations of the Japanese concerning meetings and associations were also considered no longer valid.[51] The for-

---

48 Cf. Zorab, *op. cit.* p. 62.

49 Oendang-oendang No. 23 tentang mentjaboet sebahagian larangan bersidang dan berkoempoel, *Kan Po* Tahoen 1 No. 1 2602 p. 5—6 which annulled some stipulations of decree No. 2 and decree No. 3 (of March 20, 1942, *Kan Po* Nomor istimewa, b. 2 2603 p. 9).

50 Oendang-oendang No. 21 tentang pembatasan gelombang pesawat radio, *Kan Po* Tahoen 1 No. 1 2602 p. 3.

51 See decree No. 14 of the Attorney-General, Maklumat No. 14 Djaksa Agung

mation of political parties was even encouraged by the Indonesian government.[52] And the provisions embodied in art. 27—30 and art. 35 of the Gunsei Keizirei had to be considered as having become inoperative, too, as well as the various provisions of martial law and special decree. On the other hand, many of the stipulations of chapters I, II and III of the second Book of the W.v.S. N. I. which had become ineffectual during the Japanese occupation remained inoperative. Those stipulations must also be considered as contrary to the Constitution because they provided penalties for offences against the King, the ruling Queen, the Governor General etc.

In the first days of the Indonesian revolution there was a gap in the law: an attempt on the life of the President or the Vice-President had not yet been made a special crime by the law, but could only be punished as common homicide. Even if the provisions which provided special penalties for an attempt on the life or the safety of the King, the ruling Queen, the Regent or the Governor General were still in force, they could not be applied at all to those crimes, because the words "the King, the ruling Queen or the Regent" or "the Governor General" were not allowed to be read as if they had already been replaced by the words "the President or the Vice-President". Although it had been the purpose and the idea of those provisions to protect the Head of the State, punishment by analogy was prohibited according to art. 1(1) of the W.v.S. N. I., or, to say it more correctly, according to the genesis and the system of that penal code.[53] According to the rule, *nullum delictum nulla poena sine praevia lege poenali*, a person cannot be punished according to the fundamental idea of a penal statute and to the sound sense of justice of the people as long as that action is not explicitly declared to be an offence by statute. This situation, however, did not last more than six months in Java and Madura, and not more than a year in Sumatra, and it was only due to the fact that the Indonesian legislature could not function immediately during those first tumultuous days of the struggle for independence to take all necessary measures. But it did occur a second time in the history of Indonesian criminal law that in certain regions no special criminal law provisions were available to punish crimes against the

---

tentang Kemerdekaan berserikat dan berkumpul, January 16, 1946, in *Documenta Historica,* Vol. I ed. by Osman Raliby, 1953 p. 568.

52 See decree of the Government, Maklumat Pemerintah, November 3, 1945 in Koesnodiprodjo, *op. cit.* 1945 p. 76 and Osman Raliby, *op. cit.* p. 529.

53 Cf. Van Hattum, *op. cit.* p. 74—75, Hazewinkel-Suringa, *op. cit.* p. 288 ff.

Head of the State. That second time is was not merely a momentarily vacuum, but one that lasted nearly nine years!

Beside this serious gap in the criminal law which had to be filled as soon as possible, there were many other objections against the continuation of the Japanese legal order.

First, we must bear in mind that the Gunsei Keizirei was promulgated only to be in force in Java and Madura. Consequently, only in Java and Madura certain provisions of the W.v.S. N. I. were no longer effectual. But in other regions it might well be possible that the same provisions were still left binding, while other provisions, still valid in Java and Madura, were possibly made inoperative. Since the Indonesian territory had been divided into three parts, each with its own military government, there was most likely much diversity in the laws and regulations promulgated by the Japanese for each region.

Another objection was that the Japanese legal order consisted of regulations of the Japanese military government beside Netherlands Indies laws, maintained in force by the Japanese, each of which differ in system and general principles. The validity of two entirely different systems of criminal law in the same area, binding for the same persons,[54] was very confusing, especially for the police officials who are no jurists.

In contrast to the Netherlands Indies criminal law provisions, the Japanese stipulations were considered very extensive. According to Aziz, "perhaps .... the brevity of the judicial ordinances might have been prompted by the desire to adhere to a phraseology which could be interpreted according to the exigencies of the situation".[55] The Japanese criminal law was seen as fascist law, and it was also felt as a serious objection that the penalties provided for many offences had high minima. So the judges were often compelled to impose penalties which were not proportionate with the criminal's guilt, because they were not allowed by those particular provisions to inflict a milder penalty.

---

54 Before the W.v.S. N.I. came in force on January 1, 1918, there were also two criminal codes binding in the same territory, but not for the same persons. There was the Wetboek van Strafrecht voor Nederlandsch-Indië (Wetboek voor Europeanen) binding for Europeans and persons assimilated with them, and the Wetboek van Strafrecht voor de Inlanders in Nederlandsch-Indië. But the latter was a copy of the first mentioned penal code, cf. *Geschiedenis van het Wetboek van Strafrecht voor Nederlandsch-Indië, volledige verzameling der ontwerpen met toelichting,* 1918 p. 16, also W. L. G. Lemaire, *Het Wetboek van Strafrecht voor Nederlandsch-Indië vergeleken met het Wetboek van Strafrecht,* 1934 p. 5.

55 Aziz, *op. cit.* p. 166.

The Japanese regulations were very often incomplete and gave the impression of having been made in a hurry in a period of tensions.

These were the objections felt by the Indonesian government.[56] Another objection, in the author's opinion, was the uncertainty about the question which regulations were in accordance with the Constitution and the new situation of independence and which were not. This has indeed led to the issuance of an instruction by the Attorney General which advised all police officials to consult the district attorney in cases where confusion might arise.[57]

The Netherlands Indies criminal laws, on the other hand, although also not perfect, were considered rather complete and without the defects stated above. On the ground of these considerations it was decided therefore to annul all Japanese criminal law regulations, and to restore the validity of the Netherlands Indies criminal law from the time before the Japanese occupation. It was only necessary to adjust many of those Netherlands Indies criminal law stipulations to the new situation of independence. These legislative steps were taken by Act No. 1 1946, called the law concerning the criminal law regulations.[58]

Apparently starting from the idea that the Japanese occupation of the Netherlands Indies was only effected after the surrender of the Dutch forces on March 9, 1942,[59] and that all decrees and ordinances promulgated by the Japanese had come in force after that occupation was effected, — although some decrees, as we have seen, were enacted before that date — all criminal law provisions of the Japanese military government were annulled by art. I of Act No. 1 1946, which stipulates that, contrary to the decree of the President of the Republic of Indonesia of October 10, 1945 No. 2, the criminal laws in force at that moment are the criminal laws binding on March 8, 1942. Moreover, all criminal law provisions binding on March 8, 1942, which had become inoperative since the Japanese occupation, were put into effect again

---

56 See Pendjelasan Undang² No. 1 tentang peraturan hukum pidana, Koesnodiprodjo, *op. cit.* 1946 new ed. p. 8—9.

57 Instruksi No. 2 Kedjaksaan Agung, December 20, 1945, Osman Raliby, *op. cit.* p. 563, Koesnodiprodjo, *op. cit.* 1945 new ed. p. 199 ff.

58 For the text, Koesnodiprodjo, *op. cit.* 1946 new ed. p. 1 ff, W. A. Engelbrecht and E. M. L. Engelbrecht, *op. cit.* p. 1495 ff. Karni, *Ringkasan tentang hukum pidana,* 1951 p. 164 ff.

59 See also Zorab, *op. cit.* p. 135. Cf., however, Oppenheim and Lauterpacht, *op. cit.* p. 434—435, and François, *op. cit.* p. 760, according to whom the inauguration of some kind of administration is already enough. By decree No. 1 art. 1 of March 7, 1942 the Japanese had commenced their government formally.

by this stipulation. Art. I has a double function, both an annulling and a restoring function.

Art. II annuls all regulations enacted by the former Dutch military authorities. Those regulations had been issued on base of the regulation on the state of war and the state of siege,[60] but according to the Indonesian legislature, the Republic of Indonesia was neither in a state of war with any other state nor in a state of danger.[61]

Art. III and IV give some general rules and directives in order to adjust the Netherlands Indies criminal laws to the new situation, since it was impossible to change every regulation individually.[62] According to art. III in all regulations of criminal law the words "Nederlandsch-Indië" or "Nederlandsch-Indisch(e)(en)" must be read as "Indonesië" and „Indonesisch(e)(en)". Since the Netherlands Indies laws are written in the Dutch language, these adjustments are also in that language.[63] Art. IV gives another general directive: if in any regulation a right, a duty, an authority or some protection is given, or some prohibition is directed to an official, body, department and the like which does not exist any longer, that right, duty, authority or protection or that prohibition must be considered as being directed to the official, body and department which must be supposed as having replaced the former official, body or department.

In art. V a general rule is supplemented to the other general adjustments and directives, apparently for unforeseen cases. Criminal law provisions which cannot be applied wholly or partly, or which are in conflict with the present status of the Republic of Indonesia as an independent country, or which have no longer any meaning must be considered as annulled, a rule similar to the stipulation of the Presidential decree No. 2 of October 10, 1945. Since other directives were already given and many adjustments made, it may be supposed that, different from the situation before the enactment of Act No. 1 1946, there was no longer much uncertainty concerning the application of the Netherlands Indies criminal laws.

Beside these general rules, art. VI, VII and VIII contain adjustments especially for the criminal code. By art. VI the name of the criminal code has been altered from Wetboek van Strafrecht voor

---

60 Regeling op den Staat van Oorlog en van Beleg, S. 1939 No. 582 *juncto* S. 1940 No. 79, S. 1940 No. 134.

61 Cf. Pendjelasan, Koesnodiprodjo, *op. cit.* p. 9.

62 Cf. Pendjelasan, Koesnodiprodjo, *op. cit.* p. 9.

63 Cf. Pendjelasan, Koesnodiprodjo, *op. cit.* p. 9—10.

Nederlandsch-Indië into Wetboek van Strafrecht, with the additional stipulation that the code can also be called Kitab Undang-undang Hukum Pidana, henceforth to be abbreviated as K.U.H.P. An official Indonesian translation of the code was considered urgent because there were various translations current for that name, such as Kitab Undang-undang Hukum Siksa, Kitab Undang-undang Hukum and Kitab Undang-undang Hukum Pidana.[64] According to art. VII the words "Nederlandsch onderdaan" in any provision of the criminal code are replaced by "Warga Negara Indonesia". In addition to the general adjustments for the criminal code, many of its articles are revised one by one by art. VIII, while others are annulled entirely (art. 94, 105, 130, 132, 133, 135, 136, 138, 153 bis, 153 ter, 161 bis, 171, 230) or partly (art. 139 first paragraph).

In art. 104, the validity of which has been restored by art. I, the words "den Koning, de regeerende Koningin of den Regent" have been replaced by "den President of den Vice-President". By this revision of the stipulation concerning an attempt made on the life or the security of the King, the ruling Queen or the Regent, the gap in the criminal law discussed above was filled. Henceforth an attempt made on the life of the President or the Vice-President of the Republic of Indonesia is an act provided with a special penalty in accordance with the serious character of the crime. The title of chapter II of the second Book has also been altered and has become "Misdrijven tegen de waardigheid van den President of van den Vice-President", thus no longer dealing with offences against royal dignity and against the dignity of the Governor General. Wearing a foreign decoration, title, rank or dignity without having obtained permission from the King had been an offence in certain cases according to the provision of art. 507. Now the same conduct without the permission of the President has been made a punishable offence. In other stipulations the word "Gouverneur Generaal" is replaced by "President", or the word "Directeur van Justitie" has become "Minister van Justitie", while in other stipulations "het Hoofd van de Politie" has come in the place of "het Hoofd van plaatselijk bestuur". In art. 44(3) "de Europeesche rechtbanken" is replaced by "Mahkamah Agung, Pengadilan Tinggi", and in art. 76, dealing with *ne bis in idem,* the words "of van den rechter in Nederland of in Suriname of in Curaçao" have been deleted, since the Netherlands, Surinam and Curaçao are no parts of the Republic of Indonesia, as the

---

[64] Cf. Pendjelasan, Koesnodiprodjo, *op. cit.* p. 10.

explanatory memorandum does say it rather stupidly.[65] In art. 240(1) there is no longer a reference to "art. 167 der Indische Staatsregeling", but a reference to "art. 30 der Undang-undang Dasar".

There are in all 68 revisions and annulments made by art. VIII. It will be of no use to discuss them all one by one, let it suffice to give some examples, so that the reader can form a notion of the nature of those adjustments. Some of the revisions, however, have nothing to do with adjustment to constitutional changes. For instance, the penalty provided by art. 228 has been altered. The explanatory memorandum does not say anything about the augmentation of the penalty, but it is evident that this offence: wearing badges or performing acts of some function or post which one does not hold, must have occurred more frequently during the post-war disorder and must have had a more serious nature than before the war.[66] Another adjustment to different circumstances was done to art. 234. Not only is the withdrawal from their destination or the opening or damaging of letters and other documents which are delivered at a postoffice or put into a pillar box an offence, as it was stipulated by the former art. 234, but also the same acts done with letters or documents entrusted to a courier. This was urgent because at that time many letters were sent by courier.[67]

Besides, some particular criminal law provisions were promulgated by Act No. 1 1946 as entirely new stipulations outside the K.U.H.P. which were necessary to deal with new types of criminal behaviour. Art. IX, X, XI, XII and XIII deal with the circulating of objects resembling coins or banknotes not recognized as legal currency by the government, and other crimes connected with it. These provisions were not directed against counterfeiting and related crimes, but against the circulation of the so-called Nica-money,[68] the currency of the returned Netherlands Indies government.

Another entirely new offence, penalized by art. XVI, is the act committed wilfully against the Indonesian flag which may hurt the national feelings.

Beside these new stipulations there are the art. XIV and XV.

---

65 Cf. Van Maanen, *op. cit.* p. 194.

66 Cf. M.D.B. 1953, 'Territoriale verscheidenheid van het Indonesische Wetboekenstrafrecht', p. 31.

67 Cf. Pendjelasan, Koesnodiprodjo, *op. cit.* p. 12.

68 Cf. Van Maanen, *op. cit.* p. 195. See decree of the government of October 2, 1945, Maklumat Pemerintah, in: Koesnodiprodjo, *op. cit.* 1945 new ed. p. 50, and the Presidential decree, Maklumat Presiden Republik Indonesia No. 1/10 of October 3, 1945, Koesnodiprodjo, *op. cit.* p. 51—52.

Art. XIV is a substitute for the stipulation of art. 171 of the code, which was revoked by art. VIII, but it contains the same provision as that of decree No. 18 of May 21, 1940 of the Dutch military government,[69] which had changed art. 171 W.v.S. N. I. It deals with the act of spreading rumours or announcements with the intent to cause commotion among the people, and the act of spreading news or announcing something which may cause that commotion, while it must be known that the news or the announcement is not true.

Art. XV provides a penalty for trespassing the same prohibition which had been issued by decree No. 19 of July 8, 1940 of the Dutch military government,[70] namely the act of spreading news which is doubtful, or which is exaggerated or not complete, while it is known or ought to be known that the news will cause or may easily cause commotion among the people.

In Indonesian criminal law there is a distinction between offences which form "misdrijven" or "kedjahatan" and those which are "overtredingen" or "pelanggaran", which in fact is a quantitative distinction of serious offences and less serious ones. But, as it is pointed out by Van Maanen [71] in his article already quoted before, there is no stipulation concerning the nature of the offences regulated by art. IX—XVI. Since the distinction between "misdrijven" and "overtredingen" has many important consequences,[72] it is always necessary to know to which category a particular offence belongs.

With regard to art. IX—XIII, it is evident that those offences constitute "misdrijven" or "kedjahatan", because art. XIII, while referring to the offences penalized by the articles IX—XII, does mention the word "kedjahatan". This, however, is less evident for the other offences. The only guide is the penalty provided by the articles XIV, XV and XVI: imprisonment for at most ten years or three years for the offences penalized by art. XIV, imprisonment for at most two years for the offence of art. XV and imprisonment for at most one and a half year for the offence penalized by art. XVI. According to the legislative practice in the Netherlands, and so, too, in Indonesia, a penalty of imprisonment has never been provided for "overtredingen". It must also be taken into consideration that the stipulation of art. XIV is a

---

[69] No. 18/Dvo/VII A-3, *Javasche Courant* 1940 buitengewoon no. 42 c.

[70] No. 19/Dvo/VII A-3, *Javasche Courant* 1940 buitengewoon no. 55 b.

[71] *Op. cit.* p. 196.

[72] See J. E. Jonkers, *Handboek van het Nederlandsch-Indische Strafrecht,* 1946, p. 18 ff.

copy of an alteration of art. 171, which was placed in the second Book of the criminal code exclusively dealing with "misdrijven".[73]

In the concluding stipulation [74] of Act No. 1 1946 it is laid down that the law concerning the criminal law regulations will be in force in Java and Madura on the date of its promulgation, and in the other areas on a date yet to be determined by the President. According to the explanatory memorandum [75] this stipulation was necessary because communication with the other areas was very difficult at that time, so that the validity of the Act for the other areas could not yet be determined.

Act No. 1 1946 was promulgated on February 26, 1946, and by Presidential decree No. 8 of August 8, 1946 [76] it was declared to be binding for the province of Sumatra on the date of publication, which occurred on the same day. For the other areas, however, there was no such fixation of the date on which Act No. 1 1946 would become valid. This is probably connected with the fact that the other parts of Indonesia must be considered as having quite immediately been put under the control of the returned Netherlands Indies government.[77]

Because both the temporal sphere of validity and the territorial sphere of validity of Act No. 1 1946 are determined by its concluding stipulation, the law was only in force in the territories of Java, Madura and Sumatra, controlled by the Republic of Indonesia. In the future, as will be pointed out later, the stipulations of Act No. 1 1946 will often be neglected, and so, among others, also its concluding stipulation concerning its territorial sphere of validity.

[73] Cf. M.D.B. 1953, 'Territoriale verscheidenheid' p. 31. For art. XV, in the author's opinion, it is not possible to say that the offence regulated by that article is a "misdrijf" because of its origin. The military decree of July 8, 1940 contained only a prohibition, and according to art. 50 Regeling op den Staat van Oorlog en van Beleg, trespassing such a prohibition could only be an "overtreding".

[74] According to Koesnodiprodjo Act No. 1 1946 has 17 articles. The concluding stipulation, however, has no number.

[75] Cf. Pendjelasan, Koesnodiprodjo, *op. cit.* p. 13.

[76] Peraturan Pemerintah 1946 No. 8, Koesnodiprodjo, *op. cit.* p. 122.

[77] Cf. De Jongh, *op. cit.* p. 66, Dorothy Woodman, *The Republic of Indonesia,* 1955, p. 226, Harold M. Vinacke, *Far Eastern Politics in the Postwar Period,* 1956, p. 350, Kahin, *Nationalism,* p. 145, Jones, Borton & Pearn, *op. cit.* p. 254, C. Smit, *De Indonesische Quaestie,* 1952, p. 63, Schiller, *op. cit.* p. 23. In the Linggadjati agreement the Dutch were therefore only ready to recognize *de facto* authority of the Republic of Indonesia in Java and Sumatra. For the causes, see David Wehl, *The Birth of Indonesia,* 1948 p. 74 and p. 127—128, and Kahin ed., *Major Governments of Asia,* p. 498 and p. 512.

Another important legislative measure of the government of the Republic of Indonesia is the introduction by Act No. 20 [78] of November 1, 1946 of a new principal penalty beside the penalties of capital punishment, imprisonment, custody and fine (art. 10 K.U.H.P.), namely the penalty called "hukuman tutupan" or penalty of confinement.

According to Act No. 20 the judge is allowed to inflict the penalty of confinement instead of imprisonment if a person is being tried for a crime threatened with the penalty of imprisonment, which has been committed because the offender was urged by motives which ought to be respected. It is completely left to the judge to decide, and this authority is confirmed by the additional stipulation that the first mentioned rule is not valid if the crime committed, or the way of committing it, or the results of the crime are such, that the judge considers it more apt to inflict the penalty of imprisonment.

It can be concluded from the explanatory memorandum [79] that the introduction of this new principal penalty in the Indonesian criminal law is connected with political events. It is possible that one commits a crime because he feels himself morally obliged to do so on the strength of his political, religious or moral conviction. For instance, one can adhere to a political conviction which is contrary to that of the government, and in order to realize his ideals, he commits acts which are in conflict with the existing legal order and can endanger public welfare as well. Such a person certainly must be expelled from society, but, if there are no special reasons, it is not right to impose the penalty of imprisonment upon him, since that would mean an equalization with thieves, swindlers and murderers, and he would be imprisoned together with those people. But a person who commits a crime urged by his conviction is in general not a criminal in the limited sense of the word.

By ordinance of the government No. 8 1948 [80] the necessary steps were taken to carry out the stipulations of Act No. 20: rules are given for the "rumah tutupan" or house of confinement, which are quite similar to the regulations for the prisons.[81] The differences are that in case of confinement the convicts may choose what sort of work they will do, they do not have to work outside the house of confinement, they

---

78 Undang-undang No. 20 1946, Koesnodiprodjo, *op. cit.* p. 69—70.

79 See A. van Maanen, *Een nieuwe hoofdstraf in de Republiek,* T. 1947 p. 240—241.

80 Peraturan Pemerintah 1948 No. 8, in force as from May 5, 1948. Koesnodiprodjo, *op. cit.* 1948 new ed. p. 200 ff.

81 Gestichtenreglement, S. 1917 No. 708.

may not do labour for more than six hours a day, and better food is given to them.[82] From these differences it is evident that the convicts meant by Act No. 20 1946 must be given a special treatment, different from that for common criminals.

As has been pointed out by Van der Meulen,[83] the penalty of confinement is of German origin. But in Germany itself the bill for the introduction of the "Einschlieszung" never became a law. In Indonesia it was Schepper, the first professor in criminal law since the establishment of the faculty of law in Batavia on October 28, 1924,[84] who called attention to the necessity of introducing a new principal penalty [85] in connection with the trial of the leaders of the Partij Nasionalis Indonesia in 1931, among others the present President of the Republic of Indonesia, Soekarno.[86] It is very remarkable that the words of the explanatory memorandum are exactly the same words used by Schepper. It is thus evident that the Indonesian legislature has indeed paid attention to the suggestion of Schepper. Under the Netherlands Indies government the question was already taken into consideration by the People's Council (Volksraad), but the proposal was not accepted.

Thus far the legislative measures concerning the criminal statute law taken by the Republic of Indonesia during its struggle for independence against the Dutch.

By Act No. 23 of August 29, 1947,[87] the courts set up by the rulers of the self-governing lands in Java and Sumatra were wiped out, while their jurisdiction was transferred to the courts of the government. The self-governing courts in Sumatra had applied criminal adat law.[88] Although there is not such a stipulation, it is a traditional view [89]

---

82 Cf. M.D.B., 1952, 'De Straf van Opsluiting', p. 103—104.

83 M.D.B. 1953, 'De Oorsprong van de Straf van Opsluiting', p. 103 ff.

84 Entrance into office on February 24, 1925. In June 1941 he was succeeded by W. F. C. van Hattum, who after the transfer of sovereignty was in turn succeeded by R. Satochid Kartanegara, Vice Chief Justice of Indonesia.

85 J. M. J. Schepper, *Het Vonnis in de P.N.I.-zaak,* 1931 p. 22—23.

86 See Landraad Bandoeng, December 22, 1930 T. Vol. 133 p. 608 ff. Raad van Justitie Batavia, April 17, 1931 T. Vol. 133 p. 670 ff.

87 Undang-undang No. 23 1947 tentang penghapusan pengadilan-radja (zelfbestuursrechtspraak) di Djawa dan Sumatra, Koesnodiprodjo, *op. cit.* 1947 new ed. p. 88 ff.

88 Cf. Supomo, *Sistim Hukum di Indonesia,* p. 99—100.

89 Cf. J. H. A. Logemann, 'De afbakening van de rechtsmacht tussen Gouvernementsrechter en Landschapsrechter', T. Vol. 147 p. 405: „Er wordt rechtsmacht gevestigd van de gouvernementsrechter in mindering van het

that the substitution of the courts of the government for the self-governing courts does also mean the substitution of all laws of the government for the laws previously applied by the self-governing courts. Consequently, criminal adat law was no longer binding for the persons formerly subjected to the jurisdiction of the self-governing courts in Sumatra.[90]

According to Schiller,[91] indigenous justice in the directly governed territory in Sumatra, which had lapsed during the Japanese occupation, remained inoperative. The system was not reinstituted though it was not explicitly abolished. If indigenous justice in the directly governed territory of Sumatra had indeed been replaced by governmental justice, then criminal adat law, according to the above mentioned traditional opinion, would have become inoperative, too. If his statement proves to be correct — it is conceded by Schiller [92] that little is known about indigenous justice under Japanese and republican rule — then the conclusion should be that in the territory of the Republic, the K.U.H.P. as a whole had become binding for all persons.

---

territoriale gezag, met uitsluiting van de landschapsrechter. Dat dit tevens medebracht toepasselijkheid van gouvernements materieel privaat- en strafrecht schijnt nergens m.z.w. bepaald, doch is misschien vanzelfsprekend geacht". Divergent from this traditional opinion, J. H. Carpentier Alting, *Grondslagen der Rechtsbedeeling in Nederlandsch-Indië,* 2nd rev. ed. 1926 p. 312—313 and p. 314.

90 In Jogjakarta, S. 1941 No. 47, Paku Alaman, S. 1941 No. 577, Surakarta, S. 1939 No. 614 and Mangkunegaran, S. 1940 No. 543 criminal adat law was no longer binding. In this context the disputed method of the law which singles out the regulations of the self-governing lands from adat law is followed for convenience. Self-governing courts were only maintained in Jogjakarta, Surakarta and Mangkunegaran. The courts of the Paku Alam were already abolished by S. 1907 No. 516 which amended S. 1903 No. 8, cf. Supomo, *op. cit.* p. 63 and p. 98. Schiller in his geographical table of administration of justice in Ter Haar's *Adat Law in Indonesia,* p. 31 erroneously mentions the presence of the courts of the Paku Alam.

91 *The Formation of Federal Indonesia,* p. 323 and. p. 334.

92 *Op. cit.* p. 427 note 84. Cf. Soepomo's renowned oration of March 17, 1947: *Kedudukan Hukum Adat dikemudian hari,* 2nd ed. p. 17.

CHAPTER II

THE CRIMINAL LAW IN FORCE IN THE DUTCH OCCUPIED AREAS OF INDONESIA

The sphere of validity of all legislative measures of the Republican government discussed above was limited to the areas in which that government exercised effective authority.

The returned Netherlands Indies government, on the other hand, also issued its own laws and regulations, in turn only binding in the areas controlled by the Dutch.[93]

In the sequence of events, there was a change in the extend of each territory, the Indonesian territory was being restricted more and more, while the Dutch were gradually expanding the areas under their control.

Different from the Indonesian government, the Netherlands Indies government never expressed its attitude towards the Japanese legal order.[94] In accordance with the temporary character of the legal order of an occupying power — i.e. only binding during the occupation and to become inoperative when the occupation has ended unless maintained valid [95] — it may be assumed that the Netherlands Indies government has immediately taken the attitude which the government of the Republic of Indonesia would also take later on, in February 1946, namely the attitude that the criminal law in force at that time was the criminal law of March 8, 1942.[96]

So the core of the criminal law in the Dutch occupied territories of Indonesia was also the W.v.S. N. I. In the period before Act No. 1

---

93 A different opinion was adhered to by the Landrechter of Medan in his verdict of June 9, 1947, T. 1947 p. 217 ff. Although the facts had occurred in an area under the *de facto* control of the Republic, the regulation of S. 1945 No. 135 was applied by the judge who considered himself competent since the facts had occurred within his jurisdiction (Residency of Sumatra's East Coast). But the competence of the judge to try those facts does not imply that the laws of the Netherlands Indies government were also binding for those facts, irrespective of the place of their commission. The validity of both the republican and the Netherlands Indies criminal law was dependent upon the *locus delicti*.

94 Cf. M.D.B. 1951, 'De gelding van vroeger recht in Indonesië', p. 9, R. Sastranegara, *Hukum Tatanegara Indonesia,* p. 7.

95 Cf. François, *op. cit.* p. 766, see also Oppenheim-Lauterpacht, *op. cit.* p. 437.

96 Art. 2 of the Ordinance of S. 1945 No. 122 presupposes the possibility of Japanese criminal law regulations to be maintained valid.

1946 of the Republic was put into effect throughout its territories in Java, Madura and Sumatra, in the regions under control of the Republic as well as in the areas occupied by the Dutch, there was a criminal code in force with the same name: the W.v.S. N. I. But from the beginning there were important differences. In the republican territories many provisions of the W.v.S. N. I. were not in force, either because they had been replaced by Japanese provisions, or because they had been in conflict with the nature of the Japanese occupation.

By decree No. 7 of August 21, 1945,[97] a special regulation was issued by the Lieutenant Governor General concerning the execution of capital punishment. By this new decree it was stipulated that contrary to the existing provisions, capital punishment was to be executed by being shot, unless it was decided otherwise by the Governor General. This stipulation was necessary because the other way of executing capital punishment, prescribed by art. 11 of the W.v.S. N. I., was considered impracticable in the extraordinary circumstances at that time. By this decree art. 11, although not abolished, was put aside and made inoperative.

By decree No. 2 of September 22, 1945,[98] many provisions of Chapter I of the second Book of the W.v.S. N. I. were thoroughly revised by the Dutch (art. 110, 112, 113, 115, 116, 117, 118, 119, 120, 122, 123, 124, 125, 126 and 127) while a new art. 124 bis and an entirely new chapter IX in Book III were added. By the addition of this new chapter as final chapter of the code, the total of articles was brought from 569 to 570 articles.

Because of the differences between the criminal code in force in the Dutch occupied territories and the criminal code in the areas controlled by the Republic, it seems possible to the author to state that at that time there were two different criminal codes in Indonesia (apart from the Gunsei Keizirei in Java and Madura), with the same name. A criminal code must be seen as one systematical entity, so one can consider the provisions revised by the Dutch and the entirely new stipulations of art. 124 bis and art. 570 as forming one entity with all the pre-war stipulations, which were altered neither by the Dutch nor by the Indonesian government. So it can be concluded that there was the W.v.S. N. I. with 570 articles in force in the areas of Indonesia occupied by the Dutch, and the W.v.S. N. I. in force in the regions

---

[97] S. 1945 No. 123, entered into force on August 25, 1945.
[98] S. 1945 No. 135, in force as from October 7, 1945.

under the authority of the Republic of Indonesia with art. 569 as its final stipulation.

Anyhow, it is certain that with the promulgation of Act No. 1 1946 there were two different criminal codes in Indonesia, because by that Act, as we have seen, the name of the W.v.S. N. I. in the Republic was altered into K.U.H.P.

If the opinion of the author is correct, there were even three different criminal codes in force in Indonesia in the period between February 26, 1946, when Act No. 1 1946 was promulgated, and August 8, 1946, when it became binding for Sumatra. Namely the K.U.H.P. in the regions of Java and Madura which were under control of the Republic, the W.v.S. N. I. with 569 articles in the areas of Sumatra held by the Republic, and the W.v.S. N. I. with 570 articles in all other areas of Indonesia.

On August 8, 1946, the same day when in the Republican held areas of Sumatra the W.v.S. N.I. with 569 articles was replaced by the K.U.H.P., another difference of importance was added between the W.v.S. N. I. and the K.U.H.P. Bij decree No. 2 of August 2, 1946,[99] in force as from August 8, art. 71 of the W.v.S. N. I. was revised by the Dutch. According to its original version, the principles concerning concurrence, among others art. 67, should also be applied in the case when a person stands trial for an offence, while he has already been tried and sentenced for another offence after the commission of the first mentioned offence for which he now stands trial. Since it was stipulated by art. 67 that no other penalty can be imposed together with the penalty of death or life imprisonment in case of concurrence,[100] a person who stands trial for the second time in the case mentioned above cannot be sentenced to death if he has been sentenced to life imprisonment previously. This is very unsatisfying, because if the crime for which the defendant must be tried would have been discovered earlier, so that the defendant could be tried earlier, or at least at the same time as for the other offence, the judge in that case would have the competence to inflict capital punishment upon him. Apparently

---

[99] S. 1946 No. 76.

[100] See M.D.B., 1953 'Territoriale verscheidenheid', p. 31, where it is argued that in the case concerned, capital punishment cannot be inflicted any more, because the defendant has already been punished with the maximum penalty. This way of reasoning is not satisfying, because the infliction of a maximum penalty does not prevent the infliction of another more severe penalty. Cf. the considerations of the Raad van Justitie, Batavia December 15, 1938, T. Vol. 149 p. 64 ff.

following the advice of Van Hattum,[101] the Netherlands Indies legislature, therefore, amended art. 71 by adding an exceptional rule for the case mentioned above. Capital punishment could still be inflicted, notwithstanding the fact that the defendant was sentenced to life imprisonment during the previous trial. In the Republic of Indonesia art. 71 was not revised, so the defendant could only be declared guilty, but no penalty could be imposed upon him in the case discussed above.

On July 21, 1947, the Dutch started their first so-called police action [102] against the Republic, with the result that many more regions in Java, Madura and Sumatra were put under their control. On January 17, 1948, the Renville-agreement was signed and the newly occupied areas were recognized as *terra neerlandica*.[103]

It is not certain, however, whether this extension of the Dutch occupied territory did also mean an extension of the sphere of validity of the Netherlands Indies criminal law, and thus a simultaneous shrinking of the sphere of validity of the criminal law of the Republic of Indonesia, because by art. 2 of the military ordinance of July 19, 1947 [104] called Voorlopig Rechtsreglement (Provisional Law Regulation), it was ordinated that in the areas in Java, Madura and Sumatra, put under Dutch control after that date, all existing institutions and regulations concerning the judicial organization and the administration of justice were maintained valid. Thus, the criminal law of the Republic was also maintained valid in those regions where it had been in force before the police action. In the explanatory memorandum it was explicitly said: the criminal code in force is the Wetboek van Strafrecht.[105]

On the other hand, it must be put forward that the purport of the Provisional Law Regulation was not clear at all.[106] The author may refer to art. 5 of the regulation which opened the possibility to appoint special judges in the areas concerned to deal with the crimes mentioned

---

101 In his annotation in T. Vol. 149 p. 64.

102 Cf. Smit, *op. cit.* p. 136 note 1.

103 For the map of Java and Madura under the Renville-agreement, see Kahin, *Nationalism and Revolution,* p. 233, and of Indonesia as a whole, see *Lukisan Revolusi 1945—1950 dari Negara Kesatuan ke Negara Kesatuan,* published by the Ministry of Information, 2nd ed. 1954.

104 Verordening van de Legercommandant No. 514 J.D. 1/1/18, July 19, 1947, *Javasche Courant* 1947 No. 64, see appendix of H. K. J. Cowan, 'Indische rechtsbedeling na de bevrijding', *Indonesië* 1948—1949 p. 89 ff.

105 *Javasche Courant* 1947 p. 320, Cowan, *op. cit.* p. 91.

106 Cf. M.D.B., 1951, 'De gelding van vroeger recht', p. 9 note 2.

in the chapters I, II, V, VI, VII, VIII, XVIII, XIX, XX, XXII, XXIII, XXVII and XXX of the second Book of the criminal code. According to the explanatory memorandum,[107] this stipulation was provided since the common courts, which were the courts of the Republic kept up by the Dutch in those areas, could possibly feel themselves scrupled because of their nationalistic feelings to try persons who had committed those crimes. In order to avoid a conflict in the minds of the Indonesian judges, special judges could be appointed to replace them for certain criminal cases. But it seems very unlikely to the author that any republican judge would have any objections to try persons who had committed a crime against the dignity of his President or Vice-President, which is penalized by the provisions of chapter II of the second Book of the criminal code mentioned by art. 5 of the Provisional Law Regulation. It would have been more likely if the Indonesian judges had felt themselves burdened because they had to try persons who had committed a crime against royal dignity or against the dignity of the Governor General, in case those offences were connected with the struggle for independence. These offences were also penalized by the provisions of chapter II of the second Book, not, however, of the criminal code which according to art. 2 was maintained valid in the newly occupied areas, but of the W.v.S. N.I.! The same does apply to an attempt made on the life of the President or the Vice-President of the Republic, which is regulated in art. 104 of chapter I of Book II of the criminal code meant by art. 2. Objections would be imaginable only for trial of an attempt made on the life of the Queen, regulated by art. 104 of the W.v.S. N. I. From the presence of the stipulation about the appointment of special judges in the Provisional Law Regulation, it can therefore be concluded that the Dutch military legislator had had the W.v.S. N. I. in his mind as the criminal code in force in the republican territories, not the K.U.H.P. It was apparently assumed that the criminal code valid in those territories was the same code in force in the areas previously occupied by the Dutch. The existence of a different K.U.H.P. beside the W.v.S. N. I. was not yet perceived. Consequently, the author is inclined to hold the opinion that, contrary to the explicit stipulation of art. 2 but in accordance with the purport of art. 5, the K.U.H.P. was replaced by the W.v.S. N. I. in the regions put under Dutch control during the first police action. A different standpoint was taken by the Pengadilan Tinggi Djawa Barat

---

107 *Javasche Courant* 1947 p. 321, Cowan, *op. cit.* p. 91—92.

Additional material from *An Outline of the Recent History of Indonesian Criminal Law*, ISBN 978-94-017-4668-7, is available at http://extras.springer.com

in Bandung [108] which abode by the stipulation of art. 2. For the spheres of validity of the two codes in Java and Madura according to these different opinions, see map.[109]

The amendments made in the W.v.S. N. I. after the first military action were a revision of art. 171,[110] the remission of art. 153 bis and 153 ter, and the addition of the new articles 159a and 159b, and of a new paragraph to art. 335.[111]

The new text of art. 171 was taken from decree No. 18 of May 21, 1940 of the Dutch military government, already quoted above. Only the penalty provided by the new art. 171 was much milder. Since art. XIV of Act No. 1 1946 of the Republic was also taken from that military ordinance, there was a congruency between the Dutch stipulation of art. 171 and the republican provision of art. XIV, except for the penalties provided by those regulations.[112]

The remission of art. 153 bis and 153 ter which had been intended to provide criminal sanctions against the act of propagating the claim "the Indies free from the Netherlands" [113] was apparently done because the Indonesian people could not accept those much disliked stipulations, one of which had also been applied in the P.N.I.-case in Bandung. But with the introduction of the new articles 159a and 159b the Dutch legislature in Indonesia in fact took back with one hand what it had given with the other, since the norms incorporated in the new stipulations were quite the same as those embodied in the former art. 153 bis and 153 ter.[114]

Another very important change was the change of the name of the criminal code of the Netherlands Indies government, in accordance with the stipulation of decree No. 1 of the Lieutenant Governor General

---

108 In its verdict of May 2, 1949 T. 1950 p. 14 ff.

109 Taken from a map in *Tussen Sawahs en Bergen, Het Leven van de Soldaat in de Tijgerbrigade,* p. 31. On that map a part of Madura is also shaded as republican territory, which indeed was in accordance with the situation on August 5, 1947 when the first military action was ended. But later on the Dutch troops crossed their own Van Mook-line and occupied the remaining half of the island, cf. Kahin, *op. cit.* p. 220.

110 Decree No. 5 of October 23, 1947 S. 1947 No. 180, in force as from the day following publication, which occurred on October 31, 1947.

111 Decree No. 6 of July 26, 1948 S. 1948 No. 169 in force as from July 30, 1948.

112 Cf. M.D.B. 1953 'Territoriale verscheidenheid', p. 31.

113 Cf. Lemaire, *Het Wetboek van Strafrecht,* p. 84.

114 Cf. Oemar Seno Adji, 'Kemerdekaan Pers di Indonesia', Part II, *Hukum* 1956 No. 1—2 p. 15—17.

of September 21, 1948,[115] from W.v.S. N. I. into Wetboek van Strafrecht voor Indonesië, henceforth to be abbreviated as W.v.S. I. This change was effectual as from September 22, 1948.

Other amendments were the change of the penalty provided by art. 418 from at most six months imprisonment into maximum three years,[116] and the revision of the art. 393 bis and 394.[117] But in the meantime the sphere of validity of the W.v.S. I. had been extended again.

On December 19, 1948 the Dutch launched their second military action against the Republic, which brought the principal remaining Republican held cities under Dutch control.[118] For the regions occupied by the Dutch after December 19, 1948, the military government issued the Voorlopige Regeling Rechtswezen (Provisional Regulation of the Judiciary).[119]

In art. 2(1) of the Provisional Regulation of the Judiciary there was a provision similar to that of art. 2 of the Provisional Law Regulation of 1947, but different from that article art. 2(2) of the Provisional Regulation of the Judiciary stipulated that the criminal law in the newly controlled areas was not to be applied for the time being and was replaced by the criminal law incorporated in general ordinances and ordinances of the military (of the Dutch). So, according to the explanatory memorandum, there would be no difference between the substantive criminal law in force in the earlier occupied territories and that binding in the new regions.

This deviation from the principle to maintain valid all existing republican institutions and laws had to be accepted as a provisional measure in order to prevent legal insecurity in the newly occupied areas. Suppose that the principle to maintain the existing legal order was also followed for the substantive criminal law, then, everytime before a criminal investigation, prosecution or trial could be started, one had to study first which criminal law regulations of the Republic were

115 S. 1948 No. 224 in force as from September 22, 1948.

116 Decree No. 3 of the High Representative of the Crown of January 3, 1949 S. 1949 No. 1 entered into force on January 7, 1949.

117 Decree No. 3 of September 22, 1949 S. 1949 No. 258 entered into force on September 28, 1949.

118 Cf. Kahin, *op. cit.* p. 338.

119 Verordening van de Legercommandant No. 539 of December 15, 1948 *Javasche Courant* 1948 No. 105, completed by Verordening No. 559 of August 18, 1949, *Javasche Courant* 1949 No. 71.

applicable, and what the content of those regulations was. All this would hamper the administration of justice in those regions. On the other hand, it was also perceived that in the republican criminal law many provisions were absent which were considered necessary by the Dutch, and that many republican stipulations were too severe because they were devised to deal with different circumstances, which, according to the Dutch, had to be valued in a very different way.

This time the military legislator was well aware of the existence of two different criminal codes. And again it is evident that at the promulgation of the Provisional Law Regulation in July 1947, the military legislator had had the W.v.S. N. I. in his mind as the core of the republican criminal law, and had identified the criminal code of the Republic with the W.v.S. N. I. The explanatory memorandum explained that there would be no difference between the criminal law of the earlier occupied areas and that binding in the regions put under Dutch control after December 19, 1948. But, if one follows the interpretation of the Pengadilan Tinggi Djawa Barat, this was only true for the areas occupied before the first military action. For, according to this interpretation, the criminal law already in force in the territories put under Dutch authority after July 19, 1947 was maintained valid. So, there would be a disparity between the criminal law binding in the regions occupied after that date and before December 19, 1948, and that declared to be in force in the areas controlled after December 19. Only according to the opinion adhered by the author, the given explanation was fully true.

The argument to preserve legal security did certainly also apply to the period of the first military action. If the military legislator had known the existing differences before, it would certainly also have been put forward.

The Provisional Regulation of the Judiciary, like the Provisional Law Regulation, also provided the possibility to appoint special judges, and in its system of expanding the sphere of validity of the W.v.S. I., that provision was just.

CHAPTER III

THE LEGAL STRUCTURE IN THE UNITED STATES OF INDONESIA

The recent history of Indonesian criminal law is thus marked by a steady change of the spheres of validity of two different systems of criminal law.

By the Roem-Van Royen-agreement of May 7, 1949, the Netherlands agreed that the republican government was to exercise control again over the residency of Jogjakarta, and so, on June 30, 1949 when the Dutch had evacuated the residency,[120] the sphere of validity of the K.U.H.P. comprised again this area.

At the The Hague Round Table Conference it was agreed that in the federation of the Republic of the United States of Indonesia, the territory of the Republic of Indonesia would be the same as determined by the Renville-agreement.[121] This meant a restoration of the validity of the criminal law of the Republic of Indonesia on the moment of the transfer of sovereignty on December 27, 1949[122] in all areas which had not yet been put under Dutch control on December 19, 1948. On the other hand, the validity of the W.v.S. I. was restricted again in Java and Sumatra to its former territorial sphere.

Because of the stipulation of art. 8 of the Agreement of Transfer and also according to art. 192 of the Constitution of the Republic of the United States of Indonesia, by which all existing laws and administrative regulations were declared to be maintained valid unchanged in so far as they were not incompatible with the transfer of sovereignty and with the Constitution, the two different legal orders were still binding after the transfer of sovereignty, each in its own areas.

For the W.v.S. I. the stipulation of transitional law mentioned above had another important consequence. Because of conflict with the transfer of sovereignty and with the Constitution, many stipulations of the W.v.S. I. had now to be considered as no longer binding, for in-

---

120 Cf. Smit, *op. cit.* p. 227, Kahin, *op. cit.* p. 427, Dorothy Woodman, *op. cit.* p. 256.

121 See art. 2 of the Constitution, see also Logemann, *Staatsrecht,* p. 39 note 2.

122 This may be assumed because there is no transitional law stipulation for the recovery of these areas, cf. M.D.B., 1951 'De gelding van vroeger recht', p. 10 and R. Sastranegara, *op. cit.* p. 11 and p. 10 note 23.

stance art. 104 concerning an attempt made on the life of the King, the ruling Queen or the Regent, and the provisions of chapter II of Book II concerning the crimes against royal dignity and against the dignity of the Governor General.[123] The same serious gap in the criminal law as in the first months after the proclamation of the Republic in 1945 was the consequence. But this time, different from the early days of the Republic, the legislature neglected this gap for a long time and did not take the necessary steps as soon as possible to revise the various provisions.

So, there was the very peculiar situation that an attempt made on the life of the President or the Vice-President of the United States of Indonesia was not as such a punishable offence in Djakarta according to the existing criminal law regulations in force there, because Djakarta was within the sphere of validity of the W.v.S. I., art. 104 of which must be considered inconsistent with the transfer of sovereignty and with the Constitution and thus no longer valid. And even if it was considered still valid, it could not be applied by analogy, as we have pointed out before.[124] And this is the more peculiar when we bear in mind that an attempt made on the life of the President was liable to punishment wherever committed, in Indonesia and abroad, except in the areas of the W.v.S. I., thus including Djakarta Raja, which, according to art. 68 and art. 70 of the Constitution, was the place where the President must reside. If the offence was committed abroad by an Indonesian, the person was liable to prosecution and punishment on base of the K.U.H.P., not of the W.v.S. I., according to the active nationality principle which finds expression in art. 5 of the K.U.H.P., and if it was committed by an alien abroad, the prosecution and punishment could be based on the protective principle incorporated in art. 4 of the K.U.H.P. By those stipulations the sphere of validity of the K.U.H.P. concerning certain types of crimes is extended to the whole world, except the areas in Indonesia itself where at that time the other criminal code was still in force.

If one can be prosecuted and punished for a crime committed

---

[123] Cf. Lemaire, *Het Recht in Indonesië*, p. 272.

[124] One can not be punished by virtue of unwritten principles. This rule has been neglected by Oemar Seno Adji in his postscript in *Hukum* 1959 No. 5—6 p. 47—48, who emphazises too much the transition of functions. In the author's opinion, the transition of functions is ruled by transitional law, including art. 8 of the Agreement of Transfer and art. 192 of the Constitution. Consequently, provisions such as art. 104 of the W.v.S. I. were no longer binding.

abroad, one ought to be liable to prosecution and punishment wherever it is committed in Indonesia itself without any exception, and certainly if it is an offence against the President committed in his place of residence. It is an example of really serious anti-social behaviour which is not, but ought to be a crime according to the criminal law. It is very likely that the negligence of the Indonesian legislature had been strongly influenced by the common unawareness of the existing dualism in the codified criminal law. For there are jurists, among whom some of the most outstanding, who have given the impression as if there was only one criminal code in force throughout Indonesia.[125]

This gap in the Indonesian criminal law concerning the most serious crimes continued to be unfilled during the short existence of the Republic of the United States of Indonesia. Only the regions where that gap existed gradually diminished.

On March 9, 1950, the territories of Central Java, East Java, Madura, Padang and Sabang[126] were incorporated in the territory of the State of the Republic of Indonesia, while the same occurred to the territories of Pasundan in West Java[127] on March 11, of South Sumatra and East Kalimantan[128] on March 24, and of Bandjar, Great Dajak, South East Kalimantan, Kota Waringin, Bangka, Biliton and Riouw[129] on April 4. For these areas which were called "daerah pulihan" or recovered areas, it was stipulated by Government Ordinance No. 1 1950[130] that all regulations and laws of the Republic of

---

125 For a brief review of the statements of Supomo, Soewandi, Utrecht, Thung Tiang Piet, Moedikdo Moeliono, Lemaire, and Oemar Seno Adji, see 'Aneka Warna Hukum Pidana Indonesia', *Hukum* 1959 no. 5—6 p. 31—38. However, Utrecht is well aware of the existing dualism, only he assumes that in practice the K.U.H.P. was being applied throughout Indonesia, see his *Pengantar,* p. 184 note 30, and his *Hukum Pidana* I, 1958 p. 55. This opinion clashes with his own view, discussed in the above mentioned article, where he confuses the K.U.H.P. with the W.v.S. I. since art. 124 bis and 161 bis are mentioned by him as provisions of the "KUH-Pidana" whereas those articles are absent in the K.U.H.P.

126 Decrees No. 108, 109, 110, 111 and 112 of the President, B.N.R.I.S. 1950 No. 13.

127 Presidential decree No. 113, B.N.R.I.S. 1950 No. 14.

128 Presidential decrees No. 126 and 127, B.N.R.I.S. 1950 No. 18.

129 Decrees No. 137, 138, 139, 140, 141, 142 and 143, B.N.R.I.S. 1950 No. 23.

130 Peraturan Pemerintah Pengganti Undang-undang 1950 No. 1, Government Ordinance with the rank of Law, entered into force on March 13, 1950, amended by Undang-undang 1950 No. 8 of June 21, 1950 with retroactive effect. See Koesnodiprodjo, *op. cit.* 1950 p. 165 ff and p. 81 ff.

Indonesia were to be binding, unless they could not yet be applied according to the consideration of the Minister. The existing regulations and laws in the recovered areas were declared no longer binding, except those regulations which were not in conflict with the regulations of the Republic.

Because of the stipulation of the Government Ordinance, which in fact presupposes the existence of two different legal orders,[131] Act No. 1 1946 has become binding in the recovered areas in Java, Madura and Sumatra (including Sabang, Bangka, Biliton and Riouw). In Java, Madura, Padang and Sabang it took effect on March 13, 1950, the date on which the ordinance has come in force, in South Sumatra on March 24, and in Bangka, Biliton and Riouw on April 4.

On the moment when Act No. 1 1946 came in force in the recovered areas, all changes and additions to the criminal law made by the Dutch after World War II were abolished by art. I of the Act, which declares the criminal law of March 8, 1942 to be the criminal law binding from that moment on, and the stipulations of March 8, 1942 which had become inoperative because of the inconsistency with the transfer of sovereignty and with the Constitution were restored. At the same time all changes, annulments and additions made by Act No. 1 itself became effectual, with the consequence that the W.v.S. I. was abolished and the K.U.H.P. introduced.

Act No. 1 did not become binding in Djakarta Raja, the boundaries of which were redefined and more restricted,[132] since Djakarta Raja, although a part of the recovered territory of Pasundan,[133] remained directly under the government of the Republic of the United States of Indonesia.[134] Consequently, the W.v.S. I. with all its imperfections was still binding there.

If one sticks to the explicit stipulation of art. 2 of the Provisional Law Regulation of July 1947, the recovery of areas in Java, Madura and Sumatra resulted in a change in the criminal law only in some of them, and in other areas only in some parts. Madura, for instance, was put under Dutch control after July 1947, and according to art. 2 of the Provisional Law Regulation the K.U.H.P. has never ceased to be valid there, so the recovery of Madura was of no importance for

---

[131] Cf. E. Bonn and R. H. K. Sosrodanukusumo, *Tuntutan Pidana,* 1958 p. 284/285.

[132] Presidential Decree No. 125, B.N.R.I.S. 1950 No. 18.

[133] Art. 2 of the Constitution.

[134] Art. 50 of the Constitution.

the criminal law. The same does apply to those parts of Pasundan, for example, occupied by the Dutch after July 19, 1947 (see map). According to this interpretation, Act No. 1 1946 has become binding in those parts of the recovered areas of Java and Sumatra where it had ceased to be binding, or where it never had been valid (for instance Surabaja, Semarang, Bandung, Bogor and Padang).

The State of East Sumatra was not recovered to the Republic of Indonesia, but stayed apart as a state of the United States of Indonesia. Because the greater part of East Sumatra was seized by the Dutch only after July 1947, the same problem with regard to the interpretation of the Provisional Law Regulation is present. According to the first interpretation, rejected by the author, one can state that the K.U.H.P. was in force in Java, Madura and Sumatra except Djakarta Raja and Medan with its immediate surroundings. But according to the other opinion, the K.U.H.P. was in force in Java, Madura and Sumatra minus Djakarta Raja and East Sumatra.[135]

Another important problem is the question whether the sphere of validity of the K.U.H.P. was also extended to the recovered areas in Kalimantan.

It is explicitly stipulated by the Government Ordinance No. 1 1950 that the regulations and laws of the Republic of Indonesia were to come in force in the areas recovered to it. So one could come to the conclusion that the criminal law of the Republic of Indonesia as a whole, including its K.U.H.P., was also declared to be valid in all recovered areas, including those in Kalimantan.[136] This was also the attitude taken by the then Minister of Justice ad interim before the Parliament on November 14, 1951.[137]

However, we must bear in mind that Act No. 1 1946 is of fundamental importance for the codified criminal law of the Republic, and according to the concluding stipulation of the Act itself, it is only binding in Java and Madura and in the areas for which it is declared

---

135 Cf. M.D.B., 1953 'Territoriale verscheidenheid', p. 29, Dormeier, *op. cit.* p. 110, H. J. van Schravendijk, *Buku Peladjaran tentang Hukum Pidana Indonesia,* 1956 p. 62, Utrecht, *Hukum Pidana* p. 55, Oemar Seno Adji, 'Kemerdekaan Pers di Indonesia', *Hukum* 1956 No. 1—2 p. 15, Bonn c.s. *op. cit.* p. 284/285, R. Tresna, *Azas-azas Hukum Pidana,* 1959 p. 190, 'Aneka Warna Hukum Pidana Indonesia', *Hukum* 1959 No. 5—6 p. 35.

136 Bonn and Sosrodanukusumo, *op. cit.* p. 284/285, Utrecht, *op. cit.* p. 55, R. Tresna, *op. cit.* p. 190 and Oemar Seno Adji in his postscript in *Hukum* 1959 No. 5—6 p. 48—49.

137 M.D.B. 1953 'Territoriale verscheidenheid' p. 29.

to be valid. This necessary declaration was then only given for the regions of the province of Sumatra, not for Kalimantan. Would it perhaps be possible to consider the Government Ordinance itself as the required measure to extend the territorial sphere of validity of Act No. 1 1946 to the areas outside Java, Madura and Sumatra? It seems to the author that a particular decree is required for that purpose.

The stipulation of the Government Ordinance No. 1 1950 was only to extend the republican legal order in general, in so far as its laws and regulations themselves are capable of such an extension according to their own stipulations concerning their territorial spheres of validity. If a particular regulation is issued for certain areas only as a local regulation, then the Government Ordinance may only be interpreted as merely extending the effectualness of such a local regulation to the recovered areas within its territorial sphere of validity, but not as extending that territorial sphere itself outside its original boundaries. Otherwise, a local regulation of a municipality in the Republic of Indonesia in Java, for instance, should also be considered as having become binding in all recovered areas, even those outside that municipality, including the areas outside Java. This can certainly not be accepted. The regulations of a municipality can only become effectual in the recovered areas within the territory of that municipality. But exactly the same does apply to regulations of the central legislature which have a restricted territorial sphere of validity. And Act No. 1 1946 is such a local restricted regulation of the central government. Not all regulations issued by the central legislature are designated for the whole territory of the State! Only regulations issued for the whole territory of the State can be accepted as having become effectual in all recovered areas, including the recovered areas in Kalimantan. For example, the Law concerning the principal penalty of confinement, "hukuman tutupan", has also become effectual in Kalimantan, except in West Kalimantan.[138]

So, the purport of the Government Ordinance was only to make Act No. 1 1946 effectual (again) in the recovered areas in Java, Madura and Sumatra, not in the recovered areas in Kalimantan, which is in accordance with its concluding stipulation concerning both the temporal and the territorial sphere of validity of the Act. Therefore, the

[138] Different Dormeier, *op. cit.* p. 113 according to whom Act No. 20 1946 is only binding in the areas where Act No. 1 1946 has been effectual. This is probably also the opinion of Tresna, *op. cit.* p. 189 who considers Act No. 20 as a law amending the K.U.H.P.

W.v.S. I. with all its gaps was still in force in Djakarta Raja, East Sumatra, Kalimantan and East Indonesia.

When the Indonesian legislature endeavoured to end the dualism in the codified criminal law eight years later, it was expressly conceded that Act No. 1 1946 was in force in Java, Madura and Sumatra only.[139] As regards the Act No. 23 1947 concerning the abolishment of the courts of the self-governing lands in Java and Sumatra, this interpretation of the purport of the Government Ordinance 1950 No. 1 proves to be correct. Contrary to Act No. 1 1946, Act No. 23 1947 was accepted by the legislature as having come in force in the recovered areas in Kalimantan, notwithstanding the fact that it has been issued for Java and Sumatra only. Consequently, the legislature enacted a regulation for the abolishment of the self-governing courts in West Kalimantan as a follow up of Act No. 23 1947. But afterwards it turned out that the courts of the self-governing lands in the other areas of Kalimantan were still functioning there and had not yet been abolished at all.[140]

In this connection, the opinion of Bonn and Sosrodanukusumo [141] deserves attention. Although they admit that the provisions of the W.v.S. I. such as art. 104 etc. were no longer operative because of their incompatibility with the transfer of sovereignty and with the Constitution, according to them there was no gap at all in the criminal law, since art. 192 of the Constitution had maintained both the republican and the Netherlands Indies legal order as its own legal order without any territorial restrictions. So, the provisions of the K.U.H.P. were also the criminal law provisions of the Republic of the United States of Indonesia without territorial restriction. Consequently — in their opinion — those provisions were binding throughout Indonesia in so far as there were no similar provisions available in the W.v.S. I.

139 See stencil of the Parliament No. 2575/Red/Mh, or T.L.N. No. 1660, see *Hukum* 1959 No. 5—6 p. 131—132. Act No. 22 1946, Undang-undang pentjatatan nikah, talak dan rudjuk, Koesnodiprodjo, *op. cit.* 1946 p. 73 ff, which has the same concluding stipulation as Act No. 1 1946, was also considered binding in Java, Madura and Sumatra only, cf. M.D.B., 1952, 'Islamitische Huwelijken, Verstotingen en Herroepingen van verstotingen op Java, Madura en Sumatra', p. 125 ff. See T.L.N. 694.

140 See decree of the Minister of Justice of June 21, 1954 No. J.B. 4/3/2, T.L.N. No. 641 *juncto* decree of August 18, 1954, No. J.B. 4/4/20 T.L.N. No. 642, which abolished the self-governing courts in Kotawaringin, Kutai, Sambaliung, Gunungtabur and Bulungan by virtue of Emergency Law 1951 No. 1. These areas are within the recovered areas of Kalimantan.

141 *Op. cit.* p. 286/287.

However, it seems to the author that the transitional law stipulation of art. 192 of the Constitution was only to maintain the existing laws as they were actually in force on December 27, 1949 with the proviso that they do not conflict with the transfer of sovereignty. Art. 192 was certainly not intended to effect a change in the state of affairs at that time. The absence of territorial restrictions in the formulation of art. 192 could not change the factual territorial limitedness of the laws enacted after the war.[142] And it can certainly not be accepted that art. 192 had the power to change the legal territorial limitedness of Act No. 1 1946.

According to an information of the Documentation Bureau for Overseas Law in Leyden,[143] unity in the criminal law was already established for certain persons as regards certain crimes by the promulgation of Emergency Law No. 29 1950 which entered into force on August 10, 1950.[144]

This Emergency Law defined the crimes for which certain high officials, according to art. 148 of the Constitution, had to be tried by the Supreme Court, not by a common court. Among the crimes mentioned were the crimes penalized by chapters I, II and III of Book II of the criminal code. For these particular crimes it was explicitly declared by the government [145] that the criminal code in question was the K.U.H.P. based on Act No. 1 1946. It is understandable that this was only expressed for these particular crimes, not for the other crimes defined by the Emergency Law, since many of the provisions of chapters I, II and III of the second Book of the W.v.S. I. had become inoperative because of their inconsistency with the transfer of sovereignty. Nevertheless, we must bear in mind that a particular intention of the legislature can only be binding as law in so far as that intention has explicitly been expressed in the stipulations of the law. This was not the case. In the Emergency Law the provisions of chapters I, II and III of Book II of the K.U.H.P. were not declared binding throughout Indonesia for those high officials. It merely con-

142 See also Tresna, *op. cit.* p. 192 and 'Aneka Warna', *Hukum* 1959 No. 5—6 p. 40—41.

143 M.D.B. 1953, 'Territoriale verscheidenheid', p. 30, M.D.B. 1953, 'Forum Privilegiatum voor Hoge Ambtsdragers', p. 42.

144 Undang-undang Darurat No. 29 1950, L.N. 1950 No. 54 confirmed as Law by Undang-undang 1951 No. 22, L.N. 1951 No. 117.

145 On the occasion of the confirmation of the Emergency Law as a Law in 1951.

tained the stipulation that those officials must be tried by the Supreme Court in case they had committed the crimes penalized by chapters I, II and III of Book II of the criminal code. The question whether they had indeed committed such a crime must be determined according to the existing criminal law provisions. And the question which criminal law provisions were applicable must in turn be determined by the place where the act was committed. In the republican territories in Java, Madura and Sumatra the provisions to be applied were those of the K.U.H.P. based on Act No. 1 1946. But in Djakarta Raja, East Sumatra, Kalimantan and East Indonesia the W.v.S. I. was in force with many provisions in chapters I, II and III of the second Book which could no longer be applied. So, one who had insulted the President of the United States of Indonesia in Djakarta for instance, had not committed a crime penalized by chapter II of Book II of the W.v.S. I. Consequently, the requirements of the Emergency Law were not fulfilled in that case, thus he could not be tried by the Supreme Court. The proposition must not be converted!

To end this description of the criminal law of the Republic of the United States of Indonesia, one fact of great importance must also be commemorated, namely the inclusion of the Human Rights as defined in the Universal Declaration of Human Rights of December 10, 1948 in the Constitution. According to Yamin,[146] the Indonesian Constitution was the first in the world to contain the stipulations of the Universal Declaration.

The Human Rights included in the Constitution which are of importance for the substantive criminal law — apart from those which are of importance for the law of procedure — were incorporated in art. 11, 14 (second and third paragraph) and 15. Art. 11 was identical with art. 5 of the Declaration:

> "No one shall be subjected to torture or to cruel, inhuman or degrading treatment or punishment".

The principle of non-retroactivity of the criminal law, incorporated in art. 1 first paragraph of the K.U.H.P. and the W.v.S. I., was also

---

[146] Muhammad Yamin, *Proklamasi dan Konstitusi Republik Indonesia,* 1952 p. 92. Cf. Lemaire, *Het Recht in Indonesië,* p. 124 note 4: the Costa Rican Constitution of November 1949 is also inspired by the Universal Declaration.

expressed in art. 14 of the Constitution,[147] which had the same purport as the second paragraph of art. 11 of the Declaration:

> "No one shall be prosecuted or sentenced to penalty unless by virtue of a law applicable to him at the time the penal offence was committed".[148]

The exception to the rule of non-retroactivity, expressed in the second paragraph of art. 1 of the K.U.H.P. and the W.v.S. I. and in the third paragraph of art. 11 of the Declaration, was also incorporated in art. 14:

> "In the event of an alteration of the law referred to in the preceding paragraph, the provision most favourable to the accused shall be applied".

And according to art. 15:

> "No transgression or crime shall be made punishable by total forfeiture of the property of the offender".
>
> "No penalty may cause the civic death or the loss of all civic rights".

---

147 But the rule of art. 14(2) of the Constitution is not identical with the stipulation incorporated in art. 1(1) of the K.U.H.P. and the W.v.S. I., because the first is exclusively a rule of non-retroactivity of the criminal law, whereas by the latter it is also prescribed that the criminal law must be statute law. Therefore, it is not correct to state that the rule *nullum delictum nulla poena sine praevia lege poenali* was incorporated in the Constitution, see Utrecht, *Pengantar,* p. 391, *Hukum Pidana* p. 197, Moeljatno, *op. cit.* p. 18, and Dormeier, *op. cit.* p. 114—115. For criticism, see Han Bing Siong, 'Beberapa Tjatatan tentang dan berhubung dengan buku Mr Drs E. Utrecht, Pengantar dalam Hukum Indonesia', in *Madjalah Hukum dan Masjarakat* 1959, Tah. IV No. 1 p. 29.

148 English text derived from *Yearbook on Human Rights for 1949,* 1951 p. 112 ff.

CHAPTER IV

DEVELOPMENTS AFTER THE ESTABLISHMENT OF THE UNITARY STATE

When the Republic of the United States of Indonesia was dissolved and replaced by the Unitary Republic of Indonesia on August 17, 1950 through an alteration of the Constitution,[149] the provisions concerning the Human Rights were maintained, while the chaotic structure of the criminal law as outlined above was continued because of art. 142 of the new Contitution, which had the same purport as art. 192 of the former Constitution: the existing laws and regulations were to remain in force until superseded by new legislation.

The governments of the Republic of the United States of Indonesia and the state of the Republic of Indonesia had agreed that, wherever possible, the laws of the latter be made binding,[150] but this agreement had yet to be carried out for the criminal law.[151]

Beside the serious gaps in the criminal law which should have been corrected earlier, it is indeed a very curious situation to find two different criminal codes in force side by side in one unitary state,[152] when the existence of the two separate and different codes is not based on the legal needs of the different sections of the population, which must be paid attention to according to art. 25 of the Constitution of the unitary Republic of Indonesia, and also not on differences in areal circumstances.

Why should one be punished more severely for the same anti-social behaviour when it is committed in Padang for instance, than when it is committed in Medan (see for example art. 228 K.U.H.P. and art. 228 W.v.S. I.), or why should the penalty be much more lenient (compare art. 418 K.U.H.P. with art. 418 W.v.S. I.)? The act is not more dangerous or anti-social in some regions. If one committed an act penalized by art. 171(1) W.v.S. I. in Djakarta, one could not be

---

149 Undang-undang 1950 No. 7, L.N. 1950 No. 56, see R. Soepomo, *Undang-undang Dasar Sementara Republik Indonesia.*

150 Cf. Soepomo, *op. cit.* p. 189.

151 Mahkamah Agung Indonesia, December 22, 1953, *Hukum* 1954 No. 2—3 p. 65 ff.

152 According to Ko Tjay Sing, *Kodifikasi dan Unifikasi Hukum Perdata dan Dagang,* 1958, p. 17, the existence of two different codes binding for different areas is contrary to the purport of art. 102 of the Constitution, which had ordered a codification for the criminal law.

detained provisionally by the police, but if the same was done in Bandung, the police could take that measure, because the maximum penalty provided by art. XIV(1) of Act No. 1 1946 is one of ten years imprisonment, so the requirement for provisional detention prescribed by art. 62(2) of the Herziene Indonesisch Reglement concerning the law of procedure, namely a maximum penalty of five years imprisonment or more, would then be fulfilled. Why this difference?

In case a person was sentenced to death in Jogjakarta, the sentence had to be carried out by way of hanging (art. 11 K.U.H.P.), but if it occurred in Djakarta, it had to be executed by firing squad, according to the regulation in Staatsblad 1945 No. 123. That regulation was issued because the execution by way of hanging was considered too difficult under the existing circumstances. But are the circumstances in Djakarta different from those in Jogjakarta?

According to Wirjono Prodjodikoro [153] the regulation embodied in Staatsblad 1945 No. 123 could be used for the execution of sentences of all courts throughout Indonesia, because art. 11 of the K.U.H.P. does not prescribe that the sentence inflicting capital punishment must be carried out within the jurisdiction of the court which has inflicted that punishment. So, — in his opinion — capital punishment imposed by the court in Jogjakarta could be executed in Djakarta. It is pointed out by Wirjono Prodjodikoro that the penalty of imprisonment can also be carried out throughout Indonesia. However, for the penalty of imprisonment there is an explicit stipulation in art. 10 of the Gestichtenreglement (Regulation for the prisons), while such an explicit stipulation is absent for the execution of capital punishment. The correctness of this opinion must be doubted, especially because in the regulation of the law of procedure (Herziene Indonesisch Reglement) it is stipulated that capital punishment must be executed in the presence of the district attorney to the court which has passed the sentence. Although it is not explicitly prescribed, it must be concluded that capital punishment must be executed within the jurisdiction of the court concerned.[154] Moreover, we must bear in mind that according to this opinion capital punishment inflicted by the court in Djakarta can also be executed in Jogjakarta. Anyhow, to achieve unity the legislature must intervene, which is also conceded by Wirjono Prodjo-

---

[153] In a postscript in *Hukum* 1959 No. 5—6 p. 54.

[154] Cf. J. E. Jonkers, *Het Nederlandsch-Indische Strafstelsel,* p. 15.

dikoro, who wants the government to stipulate that all capital punishments must be executed in Djakarta.

The greatest objection against the dualism is the confusion which could be the result of it, and consequently, the legal insecurity. The author has referred before to the entanglement in the collection of statutes and regulations edited by the Ministry of Information, where some provisions are taken from the W.v.S. I. while other provisions are from the K.U.H.P. One should indeed be very careful in using that collection.[155]

Because of the existing dualism, one must investigate every time whether an offence was committed within the areas of Djakarta Raja or of East Sumatra, or within the territorial sphere of the K.U.H.P. Besides, as regards the area of East Sumatra, two interpretations are possible concerning the question whether the K.U.H.P. was binding there or the W.v.S. I. (see above).

Because of the uncertainty and the confusion, there was great danger that one could be treated contrary to the law in force in that area, and there have indeed been cases in which in fact the K.U.H.P. was applied to offences committed within the territorial sphere of the W.v.S. I.[156], or in which one has used the provisions enacted by the Dutch after World War II for offences committed in the area of Act No. 1 1946.[157] These mistakes have been made by the lower courts only, not by the Mahkamah Agung, the Supreme Court.[158] But hitherto

---

155 See *Madjalah Hukum dan Masjarakat,* 1959 Tah. IV No. 1 p. 46—47 and the continuation of 'Aneka Warna Hukum Pidana Indonesia'.

156 See for instance, the Tjikini-case, *Pos Indonesia,* August 13, 1958 (art. 104 for an attempt made on the life of the President in Djakarta), and the case of Aminullah Lewa N, who was punished on base of art. 134 and 137 for having insulted the President in Makasar, *Pos Indonesia,* Sept. 17, 1958.

157 For example, the Jungschläger-case, see R. Soenario, *Proses Jungschläger,* 1956 p. 66 and p. 176, the Schmidt-case: *Keng Po,* October 15, 1956, *Harian Rakjat* and *Pedoman,* October 17, 1956 (data acquired from the Dept. of Political Science, Institute for Social Research of the Faculty of Law and Social Science, University of Indonesia, Djakarta). See for details, 'Aneka Warna Hukum Pidana Indonesia'. See also the cases tried by the Military Tribunal of Semarang on April 14, 1954 (*Hukum* 1956 No. 1—2, p. 77 ff) and on October 27, 1954 (*Hukum* 1958, No. 3—4 p. 115 ff), both with a postscript of Oemar Seno Adji.

158 See the case of Sultan Hamid II, *Hukum* 1953 No. 2—3 p. 45 which was tried *not* in accordance with the theory of the Documentation Bureau for Overseas Law (see above, note 143), the case tried by the Supreme Court on December 22, 1953, *Hukum* 1954 No. 2—3 p. 65 ff, and the case of Djody Gondokusumo, *Hukum* 1956 No. 5—6 p. 45 ff. On the other hand, the Supreme Court considered the K.U.H.P. to be binding in

no verdict of a lower court has been reversed by the Supreme Court for that reason.

Although the courts have applied the provisions of both the K.U.H.P. and the W.v.S. I. — in some cases incorrectly in respect of the territorial spheres of validity — the common practice was to mention the applied criminal code as K.U.H.P., even when in fact the provisions of the W.v.S. I. were used. This practice has probably been the cause for the opinion [159] that, notwithstanding the existing dualism, the K.U.H.P. was already being applied throughout Indonesia, as if that dualism was abolished by judicial practice.

The Supreme Court and the university teaching of criminal law have followed this practice. But in the author's opinion it is very doubtful whether this practice can be fully justified, because it can increase the already existing confusion. In his opinion the original name of the applied criminal code must be quoted, at least between brackets after the Indonesian translation.

It is pointed out by Van der Meulen [160] that art. 161 bis of the W.v.S. I. was made inoperative by the promulgation of Emergency Law No. 16 1950 on the settlement of labour disputes,[161] although it was not revoked by the legislature. Art. 4(1) of the Emergency Law permits to go on strike on the condition that the employer has been warned and the authorities have been informed at least three weeks before the strike. The trespassing of these conditions is penalized by art. 18. Consequently — in Van der Meulen's opinion — to bring about or to further a strike must also be allowed as far as those conditions are fulfilled. Therefore, art. 161 bis, which penalized the bringing about and the furtherance of a strike, must be considered as no longer binding in the areas where it had been in force previously. Accordingly,

---

Asahan, East Sumatra, because it investigated whether the defendant has insulted the President (art. 134 K.U.H.P.) or not, *Hukum* 1958 No. 5—6 p. 165 ff. This can only be correct if one sticks to the explicit stipulation of art. 2 of the Provisional Law Regulation 1947, but it is incorrect according to its system. It was not explained by the Supreme Court which interpretation was followed.

159 E. Utrecht, *Pengantar,* p. 184 note 30, *Hukum Pidana,* p. 55. Cf. the author's review article in *Madjalah Hukum dan Masjarakat* 1959 Tah. IV No. 1 p. 24—26.

160 J. D. van der Meulen, 'Artikel 161 bis Wetboek van Strafrecht', M.D.B. 1954 p. 96—97.

161 Undang-undang Darurat 1951 No. 16, L.N. 1951 No. 88, entered into force on September 17, 1951.

unity in the criminal law was achieved with regard to one act, because in the areas of the K.U.H.P. art. 161 bis was revoked by Act No. 1 1946.

However, we must also point out that art. 161 bis penalized two different crimes, a political one: to bring about or to further a strike with the intent to disturb public order or the economic life, and a common crime: the same behaviour committed while it is known by the offender, or ought to be known, that the act will cause such disturbance.[162] On the other hand, according to art. 1 sub d of the Emergency Law, the measure of going on strike, to be allowed, must be done with the intent to bring pressure to bear upon the employer for a claim. So it cannot be accepted that art. 161 bis was totally made inoperative in Djakarta Raja, East Sumatra, Kalimantan and East Indonesia by the issuance of the Emergency Law on the settlement of labour disputes. Although it must be conceded that it is very difficult to prove the intent to disturb public order or the economic life, this difficulty does not alter the fact that art. 161 bis was still in force for political crimes.

On July 13, 1951 a new stipulation was added to the criminal codes by Act No. 8 1951, namely art. 512a,[163] while on June 2, 1955 the stipulations of art. 241 sub 1 and art. 527 were revoked by Emergency Law No. 8 1955 on immigration offences,[164] which provides new stipulations for those offences outside the criminal codes. It may be assumed that these changes were to be effected in both the K.U.H.P. and the W.v.S. I., although only the "Wetboek van Strafrecht" is mentioned by the Emergency Law on immigration offences. If not, some other differences must be accepted to be present between the two criminal codes.

Thus far the developments in the codified criminal law. As has been pointed out before, in the Netherlands Indies, and thus also in the Indonesian criminal law (except during the period when the Gunsei Keizirei was effectual, see above), criminal liability of corporate bodies is in principle not known, except if it is explicitly stipulated otherwise,[165]

---

162 Cf. Lemaire, *Het Wetboek van Strafrecht,* p. 90—91.

163 Undang-undang 1951 No. 8, L.N. 1951 No. 44, in force as from July 13, 1951.

164 Undang-undang Darurat 1955 No. 8, L.N. 1955 No. 28, entered into force on June 2, 1955.

165 See the sentences of the Hooggerechtshof van Nederlandsch-Indië in the case of Spiritusfabriek Brantas, August 5, 1925, T. Vol. 127 p. 164 ff, and in the N.V. Hagemeyer-case, August 30, 1927, T. Vol. 127 p. 244 ff.

as it is done in the fiscal law.[166] According to the system of the criminal code, both the K.U.H.P. and the W.v.S. I., corporate bodies and the like cannot even be the subject of any criminal act;[167] only man can commit crimes. But this has been omitted in the regulations outside the criminal code.[168] However, although it was already recognized that corporate bodies can commit crimes,[169] and although the legislature itself had already had the idea to make corporate bodies themselves liable to punishment,[170] until 1951 only members of the board of directors or other representatives of the corporate bodies could be prosecuted and punished for offences committed by those corporate bodies. In some cases, the persons who have ordered the commission of the offence or who have directed it were also held responsible, but never the corporation itself, except in the fiscal law.

Only on September 22, 1951, by Emergency Law No. 17 1951[171] on the hoarding of goods, the legislature, who had already accepted the idea to punish corporations, has ultimately taken the last step and ordinated that in case of an act penalized by that Emergency Law and committed by a corporate body, the prosecution shall be directed against and the penalty be inflicted upon the corporate body itself and/or the persons who are supposed to have acted in the name of the corporation (art. 11 first paragraph). By art. 11(2) it is defined when an act is committed by a corporation: if it is committed by persons who are supposed to act in the name of the corporate body.

It is not true that the above mentioned Emergency Law is the first regulation of criminal statute law which enables the direct punishment

---

166 See for instance, art. 50 and 50a, S. 1886 No. 249 *juncto* S. 1931 No. 106, art. 84 and 86 S. 1898 No. 90 *juncto* S. 1931 No. 111, art. 30 and 31 S. 1898 No. 93 *juncto* S. 1931 No. 111, art. 28 S. 1931 No. 471.

167 Except art. 169 which presupposes that an association can commit crimes, cf. B. V. A. Röling, 'De strafbaarheid van de Rechtspersoon', *Tijdschrift voor Strafrecht,* Vol. LXVI 1957 p. 8 note 20.

168 See Raad van Justitie Batavia, December 30, 1939, confirmed by the Hooggerechtshof, May 21, 1940, T. Vol. 152 p. 677 ff, with an important postscript of W. F. C. van Hattum, p. 689 ff. It was about art. 3(3) Prijsopdrijvingsordonnantie S. 1939 No. 259.

169 See art. 8 Crisisuitvoerordonnantie S. 1939 No. 659, art. 21 Deviezen Ordonnantie S. 1940 No. 205, art. 12 Ordonnantie Gecontroleerde Goederen S. 1948 No. 144, art. 17 Rijstordonnantie S. 1948 No. 253, art. 14 Prijsbeheersing-ordonnantie S. 1948 No. 295.

170 Cf. Van Hattum, *op. cit.* p. 696 ff.

171 Undang-undang Darurat tentang penimbunan barang-barang, 1951 No. 17, L.N. 1951 No. 90, confirmed as Undang-undang by Undang-undang 1953 No. 1, L.N. 1953 No. 4.

of corporate bodies,[172] but it is nevertheless of great importance, because it is the natural result of the developments in the mind of the legislature as regards the economic criminal law. In this field it is indeed the first regulation,[173] and so it deserves a brief account in this outline.

In the codified criminal law the image of the criminal as "Citoyen" and "Bourgeois" is still perceptible owing to the influence of the classic school,[174] which emphasized the principle of Freedom — Freedom from state interference — and the principle of Equality. However, as regards the latter, it was only a formal, juridical equality, not a real, economic one. The real inequality of man has been perceived by the modern school of thought, commencing with Lombroso. Because of this insight, the penalties should be individualized in accordance with the needs of the criminal who needs to be helped. This is the image of the criminal according to the modern school: man who needs help.[175] The principle of Equality has lost its power. Lombroso in fact did not even see the criminal as a human being, but as sub-human, although he wrote about "l'uomo delinquente". In his opinion the criminal is not our fellow-man at all.[176] The French school has restored the human dignity of the criminal, but the abstract principle of Equality was not accentuated any more. Only the principle of Freedom was still powerful until the world crisis of the thirties, then it lost its power, too. Henceforth the principle of Fraternity has become dominating. The state has become a social welfare state, and its duty is not only to take measures in order to help the weak, but also to prevent economic destruction. Everyone must get a decent living. In order to achieve this object, the

---

172 E. Utrecht, 'Beberapa Tjatatan tentang suatu Hukum Pidana jang lebih kolektif', *Padjadjaran,* 1958 Vol. I No. 1 p. 33, *Hukum Pidana,* p. 56 and p. 96.

173 This fact has been neglected by E. Bonn, 'Enige beschouwingen over economische delicten', *Ekonomi dan Keuangan Indonesia,* 1954, Tah. 7 No. 10 p. 666, and by L. Th. Vervloet and Mohamad Jusuf, *Pelanggaran Ekonomi di Indonesia,* 1954.

174 See W. P. J. Pompe, *De Persoon des Daders in het Strafrecht,* 1928, recently in: 'De Mens in het Strafrecht', *Rechtsgeleerd magazijn Themis* 1957, p. 90—96.

175 See B. V. A. Röling, 'De Mens in het Recht', *Scripta Academica Groningana* VI, 9de Interfacultaire Leergang 1954—1955, p. 61—63, 'De strafbaarheid van de Rechtspersoon'. p. 3.

176 See G. Th. Kempe, 'Criminologie in existentialistische doorlichting', *Tijdschrift voor Strafrecht* Vol. LXI 1952 p. 170, and Pompe, 'De Misdadige Mens' in the same journal, Vol. LXIII 1954 p. 153; see also his works mentioned in note 174.

co-operation of all individuals is required. The individual has a duty to carry out in society: Freedom is not focussed any longer, but Duty. It is the image of the functionary which appeared in the economic criminal law.[177] And "c'est exactement à cause du fait que, dans le droit le plus moderne, l'accent principal est mis sur le fonctionnaire et que les fonctions sociales sont remplies fréquemment par des personnes morales, que la personne morale se trouve installée dans le domaine du droit pénal, reconnue susceptible de se faire sujet du fait délictueux".[178] Criminal liability of corporate bodies is thus directly connected with the fact that nowadays the economic functions are very often carried out by those bodies. According to Röling, it is to be expected that this criminal liability of corporations will be generally accepted in the future. He quotes Vrij who has said: "quelques unes des particularités du droit des sanctions sociales-économiques peuvent contribuer au rajeunissement du droit pénal commun".[179]

On May 13, 1955, by Emergency Law No. 7 1955 [180] dealing with economic crimes in general, the possibility to inflict penalties upon corporate bodies themselves was extended to many other regulations. In the explanatory memorandum it is also declared that punishment of corporations must be made possible since many economic crimes are committed by corporations.[181] However, three years afterwards, the possibility to hold corporate bodies responsible was restricted again to certain areas, namely the areas of the former Republic of Indonesia, including its recovered areas, in Java, Madura and Sumatra, which means a step backwards. This will be discussed in Chapter V.

To end these observations about the developments in the criminal law of the Republic of Indonesia from 1950 until the legislature endeavoured to achieve unity in the codified criminal law, a last few words must be said about the criminal adat law.

---

177 Röling, 'De Mens in het Recht', p. 63—64, 'De Strafbaarheid van de Rechtspersoon', p. 4.

178 Röling, 'L'orientation moderne des notions d'auteur de l'infraction et de participation à l'infraction', *Revue Internationale de Droit Pénal,* 27e année 1957, p. 119.

179 Röling, 'De Strafbaarheid van de Rechtspersoon', p. 30.

180 Undang-undang Darurat 1955 No. 7 tentang Pengusutan, Penuntutan dan Peradilan Tindak-pidana Ekonomi, L.N. 1955 No. 27, supplemented by Undang-undang Darurat 1958 No. 8, L.N. 1958 No. 156, in force as from January 1, 1959, and recently by Peraturan Pemerintah Pengganti Undang-undang 1960 No. 1, entered into force on February 2, 1960 (*Pos Indonesia,* February 11, 1960).

181 T.L.N. No. 801 p. 10.

In January 1951 provisional measures were taken by Emergency Law No. 1 for the unification of the organization, the competence and the procedure of the civil courts.[182] According to art. 1(2) the Pengadilan Swapradja — the courts of the (former) self-governing lands — in East Sumatra, West Kalimantan and East Indonesia, and the Pengadilan Adat — the indigenous courts in directly governed territory — must be abolished gradually on dates to be fixed by the Minister of Justice, with the exception of the Peradilan Agama — religious justice — if it is a separate part of the Peradilan Swapradja and the Peradilan Adat.[183] The jurisdiction of the abolished courts must be transferred to the local Pengadilan Negeri — governments courts — (art. 5(3)a). Since it was taken into consideration that the criminal code should be revised and adjusted to the new circumstances and that it is not yet clear whether the existing adat-offences and adat-sanctions should remain recognized or not, it was decided not to abolish them.[184] Therefore it is ordinated by art. 5(3)b that the substantive criminal law hitherto binding for the subjects of the self-governing lands and the persons previously adjudicated by the indigenous courts in what had been directly governed territory, is to remain in force for the time being with the following additional stipulations.

In case an act is committed which according to criminal adat law is an offence and which also answers to the description of any of the provisions of the criminal code, then the government court which has replaced the abolished self-governing court or indigenous court

---

[182] Undang-undang Darurat 1951 No. 1 tentang tindakan-tindakan sementara untuk menjelenggarakan kesatuan susunan, kekuasaan dan atjara Pengadilan-pengadilan Sipil, L.N. 1951 No. 9, binding as from January 14, 1951.

[183] Cf. Malikul Adil, 'Penghapusan peradilan asli, terutama mengenai Keresidenan Bangkahulu dan Palembang', *Hukum* 1957 No. 3—4 p. 7, according to whom a change of Pengadilan does only mean a change in the law of procedure, while a change of Peradilan does also comprise a change in the substantive law, an opinion influenced by that of Carpentier Alting, see above note 89. According to the traditional opinion, the substitution of a court of the government for a self-governing court or an indigenous court in directly governed territory does also effect a change in the substantive law, if not otherwise stipulated. In other words, a change of Pengadilan does also mean a change of Peradilan. The terminology of art. 1(2) is in accordance with this traditional view: only the courts of the self-governing lands and the indigenous courts in directly governed territory must be abolished and replaced by the courts of the government, not the substantive law, see art. 5(3)b. On the other hand both the religious courts and the law to be applied by those religious courts are maintained, therefore: Peradilan Agama.

[184] T.L.N. No. 81 p. 7—8.

in directly governed territory has to inflict the penalty provided by the criminal code, not that provided by adat law. Although it must be determined first whether the behaviour involved does constitute an offence or not according to the rules of adat law, the judge has also to decide which provision of the criminal code is applicable in order to know the penalty to be inflicted. In other words, he must in fact apply the rules of both the criminal adat law and the criminal code. Therefore, it seems to the author that the regulation of the Emergency Law means a step towards making the whole criminal code binding for the persons formerly to be adjudicated by self-governing courts or indigenous courts in directly governed territory.

If the adat-offence has no counter-part in the provisions of the criminal code, then the adat-penalty must be inflicted. But beside the adat-penalty a substitute penalty must be imposed which must be executed in case the convict does not comply with the sentence. As has been pointed out by Lemaire,[185] this can only be the case with adat-penalties which are not enforceable, for instance the penalty to ask forgiveness. For adat-penalties which can be executed irrespective of the willingness of the convict, the stipulation concerning substitute penalties is of no significance at all. Because of the close connection between the content of an adat-norm and the sort of adat-sanction against trespassing that norm, the adat-norm can be concluded to have no longer real binding power if the substitute penalties have to be executed very often. But on the other hand, the substitute penalties can help to restore the effectualness of the adat-norm.

The substitute penalty discussed above is imprisonment for at most three months and/or fine of at most 500 rupiah. But if the offence is of such a character that the provided adat penalty is considered much harsher than the substitute penalty of imprisonment for at most three months and/or fine of at most 500 rupiah, then a substitute penalty of imprisonment for at most ten years is provided. It is entirely left to the judge to value the gravity of the offence and the proportion of the substitute penalty and the adat-sanction. This competence of the judge to decide all by himself the limits for the substitute penalty has been felt as a serious deficiency because of the danger of legal insecurity. The possibility of appeal is also dependent on the valuation of the judge, since one can merely appeal for offences for which a substitute penalty of more than three months imprisonment or 500 rupiah fine

---

185 Lemaire, *Het Recht in Indonesië*, p. 273.

is provided (art. 6(2) *juncto* art. 6(1)a).[186] These objections are well-founded only if the judges of the government give in to their inclination of turning away from reality or if they prove to be insufficiently prepared for their task to administer justice according to adat law.[187]

So, adat penalties are fully recognized for those offences which have no equivalent in the system of the criminal code, i.e. which do not conform to the elements of any provision of the criminal code. But there is another stipulation. The last mentioned substitute penalty must be imposed directly instead of thc adat-sanctions if the latter are deemed to be improper at the present time. Thus these adat penalties, too, can be pushed aside. Nevertheless, the rules of criminal adat law are exclusively binding in these cases.

These provisions are in force for the courts of the government which have replaced the self-governing- and the indigenous courts in what had been directly governed territory, mentioned by art 1(2) of the Emergency Law. It mentions the abolishment of the self-governing courts in East Sumatra, West Kalimantan and East Indonesia.

In East Sumatra the self-governing courts were already put to an end following the social revolution in 1946, and the system was not reestablished by the Dutch. The Emergency Law has thus merely eradicated the legal grounds for the existence of the self-governing courts in East Sumatra,[188] in addition to Act No. 23 1947 of the former Republic of Indonesia which had done the same for the other areas of Sumatra. Apparently Act No. 23 1947 was not considered to be in force in East Sumatra, which is correct because East Sumatra was already occupied by the Dutch before its promulgation.

In the absence of the self-governing courts it was assumed that their jurisdiction was passed to the courts of the government.[189] It is uncertain whether criminal adat law was still effectual.[190] According to the traditional view it would have become inoperative as a result of

---

186 Malikul Adil, *op. cit.* p. 8.

187 See B. ter Haar, *De rechtspraak van de landraden naar ongeschreven recht,* oration Batavia 1930, p. 6, Ter Haar, *Beginselen en Stelsel,* p. 237, Ter Haar, Hoebel and Schiller, *op. cit.* p. 230.

188 Lemaire, *op. cit.* p. 252.

189 Mahadi, *Beberapa sendi hukum di Indonesia,* Part I, 1954 p. 262, Landrechter Medan, June 9, 1947, T. 1947 p. 217 ff, cited by Schiller, *op. cit.* p. 428 note 94. Art 5(3)a of the Emergency Law has provided the legal basis for this substitution of the government courts for the self-governing courts.

190 According to Mahadi, *op. cit.* p. 264—265, criminal adat law was still effectual because it was applied by the government courts.

the substitution of the government courts for those of the self-governing lands. If art. 5(3)b must be interpreted as requiring the effectualness of criminal adat law in order that it might be applied by the government courts, then art. 5(3)b is of no significance for the former subjects of the self-governing lands in East Sumatra:[191] criminal adat law remains inoperative. Or would it perhaps be possible to argue that it is the validity of criminal adat law, not its effectualness, which is required by art. 5(3)b? Criminal adat law was still valid in East Sumatra because its legal basis was not yet abolished, it had only become inoperative since there were no competent judges to apply it. In this opinion it would be possible to state that criminal adat law has been restored in its effectualness for the former subjects of the self-governing lands in East Sumatra,[192] because art. 5(3)b has made the courts of the government competent to administer justice according to criminal adat law.

By Emergency Law No. 1 1951 a legal basis is provided for the abolishment of the self-governing courts in West Kalimantan only, as it was apparently assumed by the legislature that self-governing courts in the other parts of the island no longer existed. Act No. 23 1947 was supposed to be in force in all recovered areas of the former Republic of Indonesia,[193] including those in Kalimantan, although it deals exclusively with the self-governing courts in Java and Sumatra. As has been noted before, this presupposition has turned out to be incorrect: in the other parts of Kalimantan, in Kotawaringin, Kutai, Sambaliung, Gunungtabur and Bulungan, the self-governing courts were still effective at that moment. Consequently, criminal adat law was also still effectual there. This presupposition is founded upon a wrong interpretation of the purport of the Government Ordinance No. 1 1950 of the former Republic of Indonesia.[194]

Afterwards Emergency Law No. 1 1951 was used as the legal ground

---

191 Dormeier, *op. cit.* p. 111.

192 Cf. Lemaire, *op. cit.* p. 271.

193 T.L.N. No. 81 p. 6. Lemaire, *op. cit.* p. 252 accepts Act No. 23 1947 to be valid for all recovered areas in Kalimantan, except West Kalimantan which, according to Lemaire, was recovered on April 18, 1950. The author has not been able to find any decree concerning the recovery of West Kalimantan, cf. Logemann, *Staatsrecht,* p. 41, Schiller, *op. cit.* p. 338 and p. 432 note 10, M.D.B. 1952, 'Decentralisatie in Kalimantan', p. 90 ff, Sastranegara, *op. cit.* p. 9. The validity of Act No. 23 1947 in the recovered areas in Kalimantan is also accepted by Schiller, *op. cit.* p. 325.

194 Cf. Logemann, *op. cit.* p. 130, Böhtlingk, *op. cit.* p. 24.

for the abolishment of the self-governing courts in Kotawaringin, Kutai, Sambaliung, Gunungtabur and Bulungan in the south and in the east of Kalimantan.[195] However, the legality of this abolishment is doubtful as art. 1(2) merely provides for the abolishment of the self-governing courts in West Kalimantan. Accordingly, the validity of art. 5(3)b must also be denied for the courts of the government which have replaced the above mentioned self-governing courts. Art. 5(3)b must be interpreted in close connection with art. 5(3)a, which refers to art. 1(2). So it must be concluded that the illegal abolishment of those self-governing courts has made criminal adat law inoperative in those areas. The government courts of Balikpapan, Bandjarmasin and Samarinda which are substituted for the self-governing courts mentioned above are not competent to apply criminal adat law. As regards the substantive criminal law for the former subjects of self-governing lands, the situation in those parts of Kalimantan resembles that in the areas of Sumatra which had been the territory of the former Republic of Indonesia. But in Sumatra criminal adat law has no longer a legal basis, it is not merely inoperative, but it has been invalidated.[196]

When the self-governing courts in Kotawaringin, Kutai, Sambaliung, Gunungtabur and Bulungan were abolished, it was expressly taken into consideration that the abolishment of self-governing courts in the whole province of Kalimantan was already possible. Nevertheless, only the self-governing courts in those five places are mentioned. Nothing is said about the self-governing courts in West Kalimantan itself.[197] Thus it may be concluded that no self-governing courts are effective any more in the other parts of Kalimantan. Then the situation in West Kalimantan is identical to that in East Sumatra with respect to the effectualness of criminal adat law (see above).

Hitherto Pengadilan-pengadilan Swapradja have been wiped out in Bali, Sulawesi, Sumbawa, Sumba, Timor, Flores [198] and Kalimantan,

---

[195] See above note 140.

[196] Cf. M.D.B. 1953, 'Territoriale verscheidenheid', p. 28, Mahadi, *op. cit.* p. 260. See also Lemaire, *op. cit.* p. 271.

[197] Cf. Logemann, *op. cit.* p. 131 note 2.

[198] For Bali, Ministerial decree of March 19, 1952 No. JS. 4/8/16, T.L.N. No. 231, entered into force on March 26, 1952, Sulawesi, decree of August 21, 1952 No. JB. 4/3/17, T.L.N. No. 276, in force as from September 1, 1952, Sumbawa, Sumba, Timor and Flores, decree of May 19, 1954 No. JB. 4/2/20, T.L.N. No. 603, in force for Sumbawa on July 1, 1954, and for the other areas on September 1, 1954.

and Pengadilan-pengadilan Adat in Sulawesi, Lombok, Kalimantan[199] and Bengkulen.[200]

As has been put forward, according to Schiller there was no indigenous justice any more in the republican-held areas of Sumatra which had been directly governed territory. Bengkulen belongs to these republican controlled areas. The presence of Pengadilan Adat in Bengkulen either proves the standpoint of Schiller to be at variance with reality, at least for Bengkulen, or it has been reinstituted by the Dutch notwithstanding their principle to maintain the republican judicial organization. Anyhow, wherever indigenous courts in directly governed territory have already disappeared, the same questions arise as those with regard to the effectualness of criminal adat law for the former subjects of the self-governing lands in East Sumatra and West Kalimantan.

---

199 For Sulawesi, decree of August 21, 1952 see note 198, Lombok, decree of September 30, 1953 No. JB. 4/4/7, T.L.N. No. 462, in force on October 1, 1953, Kalimantan, see note 140.

200 Ministerial decree of December 10, 1956 No. JB. 4/3/20, entered into force on January 1, 1957, not published in T.L.N. but in *Hukum* 1957 No. 1—2 p. 154. In view of Malikul Adil's article, mentioned in note 183 above, the Pengadilan Adat in Palembang has also been abolished. But according to a verbal information from Mr Maengkom of the Department of Justice, the decree for Bengkulen has been the last one issued on base of Emergency Law No. 1 1951.

CHAPTER V

THE ENDEAVOUR TO ATTAIN UNITY IN THE CODIFIED CRIMINAL LAW AND ITS REALIZATION

On September 29, 1958, more than eight years later, the Indonesian legislature has at last carried out for the codified criminal law the agreement made by the governments of the Republic of the United States of Indonesia and its member-state, the former Republic of Indonesia, prior to the establishment of the unitary state, to make the laws of the former Republic of Indonesia binding throughout Indonesia.

By art. I of Act No. 73 1958,[201] promulgated on the date mentioned above, Act No. 1 1946 of the former Republic of Indonesia was declared to come in force for the whole territory of the Republic of Indonesia. Accordingly, on September 29, 1958 Act No. 1 1946 has become binding in Djakarta Raja, East Sumatra (according to the other opinion: Medan and its immediate surroundings), Kalimantan (or West Kalimantan in the opinion of some authors) and East Indonesia, where it had not been in force previously.

The result is that in those areas all criminal law provisions issued after March 8, 1942 were wiped out, while the provisions which had been in force on that date, but had been invalidated afterwards, were put in force again, since it is stipulated by art. I that the criminal laws in force at present (i.e. on the date when Act No. 1 1946 has become operative in the area involved) are the criminal laws of March 8, 1942. On September 29, 1958 the W.v.S. N. I. of March 8, 1942 was fully binding again in Djakarta Raja, East Sumatra, Kalimantan and East Indonesia, but on the very moment it was transformed into the K.U.H.P. by the stipulations of art. VI, VII and VIII of Act No. 1 1946.

The codified criminal law of the former Republic of Indonesia was made the criminal law for the whole Indonesian territory. From that date on nominally one criminal code is binding throughout Indonesia, i.e. the Wetboek van Strafrecht which also can be called the K.U.H.P.

---

201 Undang-undang No. 73 1958 tentang menjatakan berlakunja Undang-undang No. 1 tahun 1946 Republik Indonesia tentang peraturan hukum pidana untuk seluruh wilajah Republik Indonesia dan mengubah Kitab Undang-undang Hukum Pidana, L.N. 1958 No. 127, also published in *Hukum* 1959 No. 5—6 p. 129 ff.

Henceforth the practice of the courts to quote the K.U.H.P. for cases which have occurred in Djakarta Raja, East Sumatra, Kalimantan and East Indonesia is entirely justified. And the gaps in the law with regard to the offences against the security of the State and against the dignity of the President etc. have been filled by the stipulations of art. I and VIII of Act No. 1 1946.

Nevertheless, the partition of Indonesia into Djakarta Raja, East Sumatra, Kalimantan and East Indonesia on one side, and the other areas of Java, Madura and Sumatra on the other side must still be paid attention to.

Firstly, for acts committed before September 29, 1958 and tried after that date all differences of the past may not be neglected.

The rule of intertemporal law for criminal cases, incorporated in art. 1(1) of the K.U.H.P., formulates the principle that no one is liable to punishment if no previously existing statute is applicable. According to this rule of non-retroactivity of the criminal law, one who stands trial after September 29 for an act committed before that date cannot be punished if it did not constitute a crime at the time when it was committed, even though it has been made punishable afterwards. The author may point to the gaps present in the criminal law in Djakarta Raja, East Sumatra, Kalimantan and East Indonesia before September 29, which have been filled afterwards by the stipulations of art. I and VIII of Act No. 1 1946. For instance, art. 104. It must be regretted that in the meantime there have been cases in which this principal rule of intertemporal law has totally been disregarded.[202] No doubt it is due to ignorance of the fact that there had been gaps in the criminal law.

The principle of non-retroactivity also forbids a person to be punished with a penalty more severe than the penalty provided by the criminal

---

202 See the case of Wahab Pena (*Pos Indonesia* of June 1, 1959) and the case of Jusuf Ismail, Sa'adon bin Mohamad, Tasrif bin Hoesain and Mohamad Tasim bin Abubakar, tried by the Military High Court, Pengadilan Tentara Tinggi, acting as a court of appeal, March 5, 1959. The author is very much indebted to the Dept. of Political Science, Institute for Social Research of the Faculty of Law and Social Science, University of Indonesia, Djakarta, for the documents of the trial, sent to it by the Chairman of the Court (May 19, 1959 No. 6/K/126/PTT). See also the case of the reporter Sujanto who was prosecuted on base of art. XV of Act No. 1 1946 for an act committed in Djakarta on January 26, 1958 and who was only acquitted because of lack of evidence (*Pos Indonesia* of the 27th and the 30th of October 1958 and of November 5, 1958).

law at the moment when the offence was committed.[203] If one has committed an act in Djakarta for instance, which had been penalized by art. 171 of the W.v.S. I. before the promulgation of Act No. 73 1958, and he stands trial afterwards, then he must be sentenced on base of art. 171 W.v.S. I., not on base of art. XIV of Act No. 1 1946 which has been substituted for art. 171 W.v.S. I. Unfortunately, there have been such cases in which the judge has based his sentence upon art. XIV instead of art. 171.[204] Similarly, in case an act has been committed in Djakarta which had been penalized by art. 228 of the W.v.S. I. before September 29, 1958, art. 228 W.v.S. I. must be applied although at the moment of the trial art. 228 K.U.H.P. has already been substituted for art. 228 W.v.S. I.[205] In this case both the K.U.H.P. and the W.v.S. I. must be quoted in the sentence, the K.U.H.P. for its rule of intertemporal law in art. 1(1), the W.v.S. I. for the provision applied to the convict.

Only if the penalty provided by the new criminal law is more lenient than that of the criminal law in force at the time when the act was committed (compare art. 418 W.v.S. I. with art. 418 K.U.H.P.), or if the act is no longer penalized at the time of the trial (for instance,

---

[203] It is not because of the rule that in case of an alteration of the law the provision most favourable to the accused shall be applied (art. 1(2) K.U.H.P.) which contains an exception to the rule of non-retroactivity, incorporated in art. 1(1). If the accused in the case mentioned above is punished with the more lenient penalty, there is no departure from the rule of non-retroactivity, on the contrary, it is in accordance with that rule, cf. D. van Eck, *Het misdrijf van hulp aan den vijand,* 1945, p. 90, Van Hattum, *Hand- en Leerboek,* p. 83, Noyon-Langemeijer, *op. cit.* Vol. I p. 62 and Hooggerechtshof, June 20, 1939 T. Vol. 150 p. 419. Retroactivity in accordance with art. 1(2) is merely prescribed if the *new* law is more lenient; this is implied in the teachings of all other authors except Simons, *Leerboek,* p. 101 and Matthaeus in the dialogue about *Nulla poena sine lege* in *Tijdschrift voor Strafrecht,* Vol. XLIV 1934, p. 3.

[204] See the case of the four reporters: Subanto Taif, Enggak Bahaudin, Abdullah Nasir and H. Sidi M. Sjaaf, *Pos Indonesia* of February 10, 1959 and the case of another reporter, Tom Anwar, *Pos Indonesia* of June 11, 1959. According to the account of the newspaper, it has been stated by the judge that Act No. 1 1946 is valid since the promulgation although at that time Djakarta was controlled by the Dutch. His attitude can be compared with that of the Dutch Landrechter in Medan, see note 93, who refused to recognize the validity of the legal order of the opponent. But the criminal law retained valid in Djakarta was no longer the law of the enemy, it was already accepted as the law of the Republic itself.

[205] See, however, the case of Moh. Noer bin Bedjo who was sentenced to ten months imprisonment for trespassing art. 228 on September 13, 1958, *Sin Po* of Mei 5, 1959.

art. 159a and 159b of the W.v.S. I.) then the judge must take his decision on base of the new law. This deviation from the principle of non-retroactivity is explicitly stipulated in art. 1(2) of the K.U.H.P.: in the event of an alteration of the law, the provision most favourable to the defendant shall be applied.

So, one has always to be on the alert and investigate first when and where the act has been committed, next, compare the provisions of the now revoked W.v.S. I. with those of the K.U.H.P. if the act has been committed before September 29, 1958 in Djakarta Raja, East Sumatra, Kalimantan and East Indonesia.

After the Indonesian legislature had at last realized the existence of two different criminal codes, each binding in its own areas, Act No. 73 1958 was promulgated with the specific purpose to achieve unity in the codified criminal law by declaring Act No. 1 1946 of the former Republic of Indonesia to be valid for the whole territory of Indonesia.[206]

But the author may call attention to the fact that Act No. 1 1946 deals with the criminal law in general, not exclusively with the codified criminal law. This is already evident from its name: the "Law concerning the criminal law regulations", and also from the presence of stipulations concerning the criminal law in general, and of some stipulations which provide special penalties for certain types of anti-social behaviour. Only art. VI, VII and VIII are dealing with the codified criminal law.

So, the promulgation of Act No. 73 1958 has its effect upon the entire criminal law, although it has been intended for the codified criminal law only. It is stipulated by art. I of Act No. 1 1946 that the criminal law in force at present is the criminal law which was binding on March 8, 1942. There is no limitation to the codified criminal law. Accordingly, all criminal law provisions promulgated after March 8, 1942 have been annulled in Djakarta Raja, East Sumatra, Kalimantan and East Indonesia on September 29, 1958. Not merely the amendments and supplements made by the Dutch to the criminal code, also not only their various criminal law provisions outside the code, but even the regulations issued by the Indonesian legislature itself after the transfer of sovereignty on December 27, 1949, and as regards the areas

---

206 See explanatory memorandum in T.L.N. No. 1660 and in appendix *Hukum* 1959 No. 5—6 p. 129—133.

in Kalimantan recovered in 1950, also the criminal law provisions enacted since 1945.[207]

Although unity in the law has been the purpose of the promulgation of Act No. 73 1958, the result of making Act No. 1 1946 binding throughout Indonesia is territorial diversity in another part of the criminal law in which previously there has been uniformity. Because of the stipulation of art. I of Act No. 1 1946, many criminal law provisions which were binding for the whole territory of Indonesia have become binding in some restricted areas only, namely in Java, Madura and Sumatra minus Djakarta Raja and East Sumatra. To give some examples, the author may point out that according to art. I of Act No. 73 1958 in connection with art. I of Act No. 1 1946, the Emergency Law of 1951 concerning the possession, the use, the importation into Indonesia etc. of fire arms, ammunition and other explosives [208] has ceased to be binding in Djakarta Raja, East Sumatra, Kalimantan and East Indonesia. The regulation which had been binding on March 8, 1942 has been substituted for the Emergency Law of 1951, since art. I of Act No. 1 1946 has a double function. The penalties provided by the regulation now in force again are much more lenient. These penalties must be inflicted for the illegal possession of fire-arms after September 29, 1958.[209] And it might even be stated that these penalties must be inflicted for acts committed before September 29, 1958, but tried afterwards.[210]

Different from the Emergency Law of 1951, before the war no penalty was provided for the possession of swords and the like. Accordingly, it does no longer constitute a crime in Djakarta Raja, East Sumatra, Kalimantan and East Indonesia.[211] Similarly, the above mentioned regulations of economic criminal law are invalidated in

---

207 For instance, the Law concerning the "hukuman tutupan", see note 138. In Peraturan Pemerintah 1959 No. 56, L.N. 1959 No. 134 it is assumed that the Law concerning the "hukuman tutupan" is in force for the whole Indonesian territory.

208 Undang-undang Darurat 1951 No. 12, L.N. 1951 No. 78.

209 Vuurwapenregeling 1936, S. 1937 No. 170 *juncto* S. 1939 No. 278 and No. 280. See, however, the trial of Pudin bin Sawiri, Djaumhari bin Saleh and Ismail bin Djasria, *Pedoman* of June 13, 1959. See also the case reported by *Pos Indonesia* of August 8, 1959.

210 See, however, the trial of Wahab Pena, Jusuf Ismail, Sa'adon bin Mohamad, Tasrif bin Hoesain and Tasim bin Abubakar, note 202, and of Rachman bin Moestapa (*Pos Indonesia,* December 30, 1958) and of Siman bin Kuat (*Pos Indonesia,* December 20, 1958).

211 See, however, the announcement of the authorities, in *Pos Indonesia* of May 15, 1959.

those areas.[212] Henceforth, corporate bodies are not liable to punishment any more in Djakarta Raja, East Sumatra, Kalimantan and East Indonesia. And the additional stipulations of Emergency Law No. 1 1951 concerning the criminal adat law discussed above must also be considered as no longer binding in the regions of East Sumatra, Kalimantan and East Indonesia. They are only still in force for the persons formerly submitted to the jurisdiction of the Pengadilan Adat in the areas of the former Republic of Indonesia in Sumatra, i.e. Sumatra except East Sumatra. This, provided that the laws are now directly binding for the (former) subjects of the self-governing lands and the autochthonous population in what had been directly governed territory with indigenous justice. But that is still a question.

It is clear that the legislature has entirely neglected the further consequences of art. I of Act No. 1 1946. Nevertheless, the explicit stipulations of art. I of Act No. 73 1958 and art. I of Act No. 1 1946 must be accepted as having effected this new territorial diversity of the criminal law, since no other interpretation is possible for those stipulations. It is not allowed to abide by the intention of the legislature if it is not in accordance with the words used to formulate that intention.

If one would like to deny the double function of art. I of Act No. 1 1946,[213] then it should be both for the codified and for the uncodified criminal law, because art. I does not discriminate between codified and uncodified criminal law. It deals with the criminal law in general.

And if the function of art. I would be denied for the sake of the uncodified criminal law, it should be concluded that the legislature's endeavour to achieve unity for the codified criminal law has been a

---

212 Uniform penalties for the whole territory of Indonesia are provided again by Presidential Decree, Penetapan Presiden 1959 No. 5, L.N. 1959 No. 80 (a penalty of *at least* one year imprisonment or at most imprisonment for 20 years, or imprisonment for life or capital punishment, with the special requirement that the offender knows or ought to know, that his economic crime will disturb the achievement of the government's program) and by Government Ordinance with the rank of Law, Peraturan Pemerintah Pengganti Undang-undang 1959 No. 21, L.N. 1959 No. 130 which prescribes the infliction of both imprisonment and fine cumulatively.

213 Cf. Oemar Seno Adji in his postscript in *Hukum* 1959 No. 5—6, p. 51. But on p. 45 it is stated that after the promulgation of Act No. 73 1958 the problems discussed in 'Aneka Warna Hukum Pidana Indonesia' will no longer arise, which is in contradiction with his reluctance to accept art. I of Act No. 1 1946 in its double function. Moreover, he erroneously cites September 20, 1958 as the date of promulgation of Act No. 73 1958.

total failure. Although art. VIII of Act No. 1 1946 has altered the provisions of art. 110, 112, 117, 122 and 123, the penalties provided by those stipulations would still be different for Djakarta Raja, East Sumatra, Kalimantan and East Indonesia. Likewise, the stipulations of art. 71, 113, 115, 116, 117, 118, 119, 120, 124, 125, 126, 127, 335, 393 bis, 394 and 418 would remain different from the provisions binding in Java, Madura and Sumatra minus Djakarta Raja and East Sumatra. And art. 124 bis, 159a, 159b and 570 would also be still in force in Djakarta Raja, East Sumatra, Kalimantan and East Indonesia. Moreover, all previous gaps in the law with respect to the crimes against the security of the State and against the dignity of the President of the Republic of Indonesia can only be filled by both art. I and art. VIII. In order that stipulations such as art. 104, which had been invalidated because of their inconsistency with the transfer of sovereignty, might be changed by art. VIII, they should be put in force first. It is not possible to change a non-existing stipulation. Art. I is indispensable to achieve unity of the codified criminal law by making Act No. 1 1946 binding for the whole territory of Indonesia. But at the same time it has caused another territorial diversity.

Six weeks after the promulgation of Act No. 73 1958 the author has already stressed the necessity for the Indonesian legislature to take immediately the legislative steps to correct this mistake.[214] Otherwise, either many types of criminal behaviour will escape punishment, or the practice of the courts in the areas involved will be contrary to the stipulation of art. 1 of the K.U.H.P. by punishing acts for which there is no longer any criminal law provision available, or by inflicting penalties which exceed the limits.

To achieve unity for the codified criminal law, for which Act No. 73 1958 is intended, instead of extending the validity of Act No. 1 1946, it would have been better to declare the K.U.H.P. as such to be in force throughout Indonesia, while the W.v.S. I. must be revoked in the areas where it had been in force. By doing so, the trouble caused by art. I of Act No. 1 1946 could have been avoided. But exactly the stipulation of art. I has been entirely neglected by the legislature, as it has often happened before.

Beside the replacement of the W.v.S. I. by the K.U.H.P. in the way proposed above, the particular stipulations of art. IX, X, XI, XII,

---

[214] In his review-article of November 12, 1958, *Madjalah Hukum dan Masjarakat* 1959 No. 1 p. 27—28.

XIII, XIV and XV should be made stipulations of the criminal code itself, together with the new provisions introduced by Act No. 73 1958. Then there would be no longer any doubt about the question whether those offences constitute "misdrijven" or "overtredingen". The placement in the second Book or in the third Book of the code would decide that question. Art. IV and V of Act No. 1 1946 could also be included in the regulation needed for the substitution of the K.U.H.P. for the W.v.S. I. Art. II is unnecessary because there are no longer any regulations of the former Dutch military government binding in Indonesia,[215] and so is art. III because in Djakarta Raja, East Sumatra, Kalimantan and East Indonesia there is already the Ordinance of September 21, 1948 with a similar stipulation.

The question may also be asked whether all criminal law provisions promulgated by the Dutch after 1942 and before December 27, 1949 should not be investigated minutely one by one in order to decide whether a regulation should be annulled or be made binding for the whole territory of Indonesia, as has been done with the various tax-regulations immediately after the transfer of sovereignty.[216] Without the stipulation of art. I of Act No. 1 1946 this question must be taken into consideration.

On the other hand it is necessary to make many criminal law provisions of the former Republic of Indonesia binding for the entire territory of Indonesia, for instance the law concerning the penalty of confinement which until now is only in force in certain regions.[217]

It must also be regretted that the legislature did not take the opportunity to alter art. 71 of the K.U.H.P. It would have been better to take over the stipulation of the now abolished art. 71 of the W.v.S. I.

By declaring the K.U.H.P. — as it was binding in Java, Madura and Sumatra with the exception of Djakarta Raja and East Sumatra on September 28, 1958 — to be in force for the whole of Indonesia instead of making Act No. 1 1946 binding in Djakarta Raja, East Sumatra,

---

215 The author has overlooked this fact in 'Aneka Warna Hukum Pidana Indonesia', cf. Undang-undang Keadaan Bahaja 1957 No. 74, L.N. 1957 No. 160 art. 60.

216 See Undang-undang Darurat 1950 No. 36, L.N. 1950 No. 78, confirmed as Undang-undang by Undang-undang 1952 No. 4 L.N. 1952 No. 43. The various regulations concerning the economic criminal law issued by the Dutch must also be considered as having been extended in their validity by Undang-undang Darurat 1955 No. 7, see note 180.

217 See note 207.

Kalimantan and East Indonesia, another odd consequence of art. I of Act No. 1 1946 would have been avoided which is the third reason why the division of the Indonesian territory into Djakarta Raja, East Sumatra, Kalimantan and East Indonesia on one hand and the remaining areas on the other hand must still be paid attention to.

Art. I of Act No. 1 1946 is a requisite in order that the legislature might succeed for the greater part in its endeavour to attain the purpose of Act No. 73 1958, i.e. unity for the codified criminal law, but it is also on account of that very stipulation that the legislature has not completely achieved its purpose. It would have been achieved if the legislature's assumption that the K.U.H.P. — as it was binding before the promulgation of Act No. 73 1958 on September 29, 1958 — is exclusively based on Act No. 1 1946 [218] had been true. But this is not the case. As has been pointed out, a new art. 512a was added by Act No. 8 1951, while art. 241 sub 1 and art. 527 were revoked by Emergency Law No. 8 1955. Because of art. I of Act No. 1 1946, art. 512a has been annulled again in Djakarta Raja, East Sumatra, Kalimantan and East Indonesia on September 29, 1958, and art. 241 sub 1 and art. 527 have been restored as being stipulations of March 8, 1942. Although nominally only one criminal code is in force throughout Indonesia, substantially there are still a few differences left. It can be stated that there is one K.U.H.P. with art. 512a and without art. 241 sub 1 and art. 527 in Java, Madura and Sumatra minus Djakarta Raja and East Sumatra, and one without art. 512a but with art. 241 sub 1 and art. 527 in Djakarta Raja, East Sumatra, Kalimantan and East Indonesia. In the latter areas the criminal law provisions of Emergency Law No. 8 1955 itself which had replaced art. 241 sub 1 and art. 527 no longer valid. The provisions concerning the immigration offences are only binding in the areas of the former Republic of Indonesia in Java, Madura and Sumatra.

Apart from the codified criminal law for which unity has been all but achieved and apart from the criminal law provisions embodied in Act No. 1 1946 itself, in another respect unity has been effected by

---

[218] Cf. art. III of Act No. 73 1958: "Kitab Undang-undang Hukum Pidana (Staatsblad 1915 No. 732) seperti beberapa kali diubah, dan *terachir* oleh Undang-undang No. 1 tahun 1946 Republik Indonesia . . . . " (italics of the author). In 'Aneka Warna Hukum Pidana Indonesia' the author has taken this stipulation at its face value. So he did not yet perceive the fact that the legislature has not achieved its purpose completely.

the promulgation of Act No. 73 1958, namely for the law concerning the execution of capital punishment.[219]

It is true that the regulation in Staatsblad 1945 No. 123 concerning the execution of capital punishment by being shot is in fact not a rule of substantive criminal law, but one belonging to the law of procedure because it merely regulates the way of carrying out a sentence, and it is also true that Act No. 1 1946 is designated to deal with the substantive criminal law only,[220] but in the author's opinion the regulation in Staatsblad 1945 No. 123 must nevertheless be considered as being intended to belong to the material sphere of validity of Act No. 1 1946. The author may remind the reader that a similar regulation was present in art. 5 of the Gunsei Keizirei, while it can certainly not be denied that this Japanese regulation concerning the execution of capital punishment was also intended to be annulled by art. I of Act No. 1 1946.[221] Art. 11 of the K.U.H.P. does also contain this rule concerning the execution of capital punishment, while it is not regulated in the law of procedure.[222] Accordingly, the regulation in Staatsblad 1945 No. 123 must also be considered as annulled by art. I of Act No. 1 1946 and replaced by the stipulation of art. 11 of the K.U.H.P. which is a stipulation of March 8, 1942. Henceforth, capital punishment throughout Indonesia has to be carried out by hanging. However, the effect of Act No. 73 1958 via Act No. 1 1946 as regards the execution of capital punishment has not yet been realized by most jurists.[223]

In connection with the promulgation of Government Ordinances concerning the National Flag of the Republic of Indonesia, the use of

---

219 The effect of the promulgation of Act No. 73 1958 as regards the regulation of S. 1945 No. 123 is not accepted by Wirjono Prodjodikoro in his postscript in *Hukum* 1959 No. 5—6 p. 54, which is due to the fact that he does not see the further consequences of making Act No. 1 1946 binding for Djakarta Raja, East Sumatra, Kalimantan and East Indonesia.

220 See Pendjelasan Undang-undang No. 1 tentang Peraturan Hukum Pidana, Koesnodiprodjo, *op. cit.* 1946 p. 9.

221 The Gunsei Keizirei was intended to be eliminated as a whole, see Koesnodiprodjo, *ibid.*

222 Cf. Jonkers, *op. cit.* p. 15: "De *wijze* van ten uitvoerlegging der doodstraf is geregeld in het materieele strafrecht". See also J. M. van Bemmelen, *Strafvordering, Leerboek van het Nederlandse strafprocesrecht,* 6th rev. ed. 1957 p. 7.

223 See the statements of the Pengadilan Negeri Djakarta (*Pos Indonesia,* February 24, 1959), of the Pengadilan Tentara Tinggi (*Pos Indonesia,* March 7, 1959), of the Attorney General (*Pos Indonesia,* September 5, 1959) and of the Chief Justice of Indonesia (*Pos Indonesia,* March 12, 1959) (see also note 219).

the State's symbol and the use of foreign national flags in Indonesia,[224] three new articles are inserted into the K.U.H.P. by Act No. 73 1958.

According to art. 52a, placed after art. 52 in the K.U.H.P. concerning the augmentation of punishment for crimes committed by public officials, the penalty provided for a "kedjahatan" can be augmented with one third in case the Indonesian National Flag is used at the time of the offence, because it is possible that the National Flag is used in order to facilitate the commission of the crime, or that one is impressed by the use of the Flag and thinks that the perpetrator is acting officially and thus lawfully.

Art. 142a provides a penalty for the person who taunts the national flag of a friendly nation, while by art. 154a a penalty is provided for the person who taunts the Indonesian Flag or the Indonesian State-symbol. In connection, art. XVI of Act No. 1 1946 has been revoked.

The new provisions are taken from the military criminal code. According to the general considerations, art. XVI had to be replaced, since art. XVI was only in force in Java, Madura and Sumatra.[225] Now that there is a Government Ordinance concerning the Indonesian National Flag, it was considered necessary to issue a criminal law provision for the whole territory of Indonesia. This explanation is rather curious, since art. XVI would also have become binding throughout Indonesia by making Act No. 1 1946 valid for the whole Indonesian territory, if it had not been abolished. More plausible is the other explanation given by the explanatory memorandum. Art. XVI provided a penalty for the person who intentionally commits an act against the Indonesian Flag which can insult the national feelings. However, it is very difficult to determine whether this requirement has actually been fulfilled.

It is also incomprehensible why the stipulation replacing art. XVI of Act No. 1 1946 has been placed in the criminal code, while art. IX, X, XI, XII, XIII, XIV and XV are left outside the code.

While some new criminal law stipulations are provided by art. III of Act No. 73 1958 as additions to the criminal law provisions of the Government Ordinances mentioned above against the trespassing of

---

224 Peraturan Pemerintah 1958 No. 40 L.N. 1958 No. 68, Peraturan Pemerintah 1958 No. 43, L.N. 1958 No. 71 and Peraturan Pemerintah 1958 No. 41, L.N. 1958 No. 69, in force as from July 10, 1958.

225 See explanatory memorandum; it is more correct to say: in the areas of the former Republic of Indonesia in Java, Madura and Sumatra = Java, Madura and Sumatra minus Djakarta Raja and East Sumatra.

the regulations concerning the use of the Indonesian National Flag, the Indonesian State-symbol and foreign national flags, these criminal law provisions themselves have been invalidated in Djakarta Raja, East Sumatra, Kalimantan and East Indonesia because of art. I of Act No. 73 1958 via art. I of Act. No. 1 1946.

Too short a time has lapsed since Indonesia's return to the Constitution of 1945 to give an objective account of the further developments of the Indonesian criminal law.[226] The author may therefore conclude this outline with expressing the hope that the legislature will soon reconsider its rather thoughtless enactment of September 29, 1958, for instance by making art. 512a and all other criminal law provisions outside the criminal code which were in force on September 28, 1958, operative again for Djakarta Raja, East Sumatra, Kalimantan and East Indonesia, while on the other hand art. 241 sub 1 and art. 527 must be revoked in those areas. Until now, however, there are no signs yet which point out that the legislature is already aware of its mistake. And as long as the legislature does not realize it, no corrections can be expected.

---

[226] Suffice it to mention only some new regulations, see note 180 and note 212. By Undang-undang No. 1 1960, art. 359, 360 and 188 of the K.U.H.P. have been revised (*Pos Indonesia* of March 12, 1960). It is very curious that the penalties now provided by art. 359 and art. 360(1) are the same. By Peraturan Pemerintah Pengganti Undang-undang No. 16 1960 the requirement of 25 guilders in art. 364, 373, 379, 384 and 407 has been altered into 250 rupiah (*Pos Indonesia,* April 19, 1960). By Peraturan Pemerintah Pengganti Undang-undang No. 18 1960 all fines provided by the provisions of the K.U.H.P. and all other criminal law provisions promulgated before August 17, 1945, except the provisions of the economic criminal law, have been augmented (*Pos Indonesia,* April 20, 1960).

LITERATURE CITED

Aziz, M. A., *Japan's Colonialism and Indonesia* (1955).

Bemmelen, J. M. van, *Strafvordering, Leerboek van het Nederlandse Strafprocesrecht* (zesde herz. dr. 1957).

Bemmelen, J. M. van, Erkent de Hoge Raad thans Voorwaardelijk Opzet? in *Nederlands Juristenblad* 1955.

Böhtlingk, F. R., *Staatsrecht in Indonesië 1942—1951* (stencil 1951).

Bonn, E., Enige beschouwingen over economische delicten, in *Ekonomi dan Keuangan Indonesia* Tah. 7 No. 10 (1954).

Bonn, E. dan R. H. K. Sosrodanukusumo, *Tuntutan Pidana* (1958).

Carpentier Alting, J. H., *Grondslagen der Rechtsbedeeling in Nederlandsch-Indië* (tweede geheel herziene uitgaaf 1926).

Cowan, H. K. J., Indische Rechtsbedeling na de bevrijding, in *Indonesië,* 2de Jaargang 1948—1949.

Cremers, P. F. A., *Het Transitoire Strafrecht,* diss. Leiden (1884).

Decentralisatie in Kalimantan, in *Mededelingen van het Documentatiebureau voor Overzees Recht,* Leiden 2de Jrg. 1952.

Djojodiguno, M. M., Membaiki salah paham, in *Hukum* 1957 No. 1—2.

Dormeier, J. J., *Pengantar Ilmu Hukum,* II (1955).

Eck, D. van, *Het Misdrijf van hulp aan den vijand* (1945).

Edwards, J. Ll. J., *Mens Rea in Statutory Offences* (1955).

Engelbrecht, W. A. & E. M. L. Engelbrecht, *Kitab² Undang², Undang² dan Peraturan² serta Undang² Dasar Sementara Republik Indonesia* (1956).

Forum Privilegiatum voor hoge ambtsdragers, in *Mededelingen van het Documentatiebureau voor Overzees Recht,* Leiden 3de Jrg. 1953.

François, J. P. A., *Grondlijnen van het Volkenrecht* (1954).

De Gelding van vroeger recht in Indonesië, in *Mededelingen van het Documentatiebureau voor Overzees Recht,* Leiden 1ste Jrg. 1951.

Geschiedenis van het Wetboek van Strafrecht voor Nederlandsch Indië, Volledige Verzameling der ontwerpen met Toelichting en de ter zake uitgebrachte adviezen (1918).

Guggenheim, P., *Lehrbuch des Völkerrechts,* II (1951).

Haar, B. ter, *Beginselen en Stelsel van het Adatrecht* (vierde ongewijzigde druk 1950).

Haar, B. ter, *Adat Law in Indonesia,* translated from the Dutch and edited with an introduction by E. A. Hoebel and A. A. Schiller (1948).

Haar, B. ter, *De Rechtspraak van de Landraden naar ongeschreven recht,* Rede Batavia 28 October 1930.

Hamel, G. A. van, *Inleiding tot de Studie van het Nederlandsche Strafrecht* (vierde dr. bijgew. door J. V. van Dijck 1927).

Han Bing Siong, Beberapa Tjatatan tentang dan berhubung dengan buku Mr Drs E. Utrecht, Pengantar dalam Hukum Indonesia, in *Madjalah Hukum dan Masjarakat* Tah. IV No. 1 1959.

Han Bing Siong, Aneka Warna Hukum Pidana Indonesia (Berkenaan dengan diundangkannja Undang[2] No. 73 1958), in *Hukum* 1959 No. 5—6.
Han Tiauw Hing, Overzicht van de Rechtspraak tijdens de Japanse Bezetting, in *Mededelingen van de Chinese Juristenkring* 1948 No. 4 (stencil).
Hattum, W. F. C. van, *Hand- en Leerboek van het Nederlandse Strafrecht,* Deel I (1953).
Hattum, W. F. C. van, postscripts in *Indisch Tijdschrift van het Recht,* Deel 149 p. 64, Deel 152 p. 689 ff.
Hazewinkel-Suringa, D., *Inleiding tot de Studie van het Nederlandse Strafrecht* (2de dr. 1956).

Idema, H. A., *De Indische Wetboeken van Strafrecht 1848—1934* (1934).
Islamitische Huwelijken, Verstotingen en Herroepingen van Verstotingen op Java, Madura en Sumatra, in *Mededelingen van het Documentatiebureau voor Overzees Recht,* Leiden 2de Jrg. 1952.

Jones, F. C., *Japan's New Order in East Asia 1937—1945* (1954).
Jones, F. C., Hugh Borton & B. Pearn, *The Far East 1942—1946* (1955).
Jongh, J. J. de, *Het Nieuwe Cassatie-instituut van Indonesië,* diss. Djakarta 1951.
Jonkers, J. E., *Het Nederlandsch-Indische Strafstelsel* (1940).
Jonkers, J. E., *Handboek van het Nederlandsch-Indische Strafrecht* (1946).

Kahin, G. McT., *Nationalism and Revolution in Indonesia* (1952).
Kahin, G. McT., ed., *Major Governments of Asia* (1958).
Karni, *Ringkasan tentang Hukum Pidana* (1951).
Kartodirdjo, Oerip, De Rechtspraak op Java en Madoera tijdens de Japanse Bezetting 1942—1945, in *Tijdschrift van het Recht* 1947.
Kelsen, Hans, *Principles of International Law* (2nd ed. 1956).
Kempe, G. Th., Criminologie in existentialistische doorlichting, in *Tijdschrift voor Strafrecht,* Deel LXI 1952.
Ko Tjay Sing, *Kodifikasi dan Unifikasi Hukum Perdata dan Dagang,* Semarang 1958.
Koesnodiprodjo, *Himpunan Undang[2], Peraturan[2], Penetapan[2] Pemerintah Republik Indonesia* (penerbitan baru) 1945, 1946, 1947, 1948, 1950.
Kollewijn, R. D. en R. van Dijk, *Staatsrecht en Rechterlijke Organisatie van Indonesië in Overgangstijd,* stencil (2de dr. 1950).

Lemaire, W. L. G., *Het Wetboek van Strafrecht voor Nederlandsch-Indië vergeleken met het Nederlandsche Wetboek van Strafrecht* (1934).
Lemaire, W. L. G., *Het Recht in Indonesië, Hukum Indonesia* (2de dr. 1955).
Logemann, J. H. A., De Afbakening van de Rechtsmacht tussen Gouvernementsrechter en Landschapsrechter, in *Indisch Tijdschrift van het Recht,* Deel 147.
Logemann, J. H. A., *Het Staatsrecht van Indonesië* (3de herz. dr. 1955).
Logemann, J. H. A., Rechter en Administratie overzee, in *Rechtsgeleerd magazijn Themis* 1957.
Lukisan Revolusi 1945—1950 dari Negara Kesatuan ke Negara Kesatuan (Kementerian Penerangan Republik Indonesia tjet. ke-2 1954).

Maanen, A. van, Het Strafrecht van de Republiek, in *Tijdschrift van het Recht* 1947.
Maanen, A. van, Een nieuwe hoofdstraf in de Republiek, in *Tijdschrift van het Recht* 1947.

Mahadi, *Beberapa Sendi Hukum di Indonesia,* I (1954).
Malikul Adil, Penghapusan Peradilan Asli, terutama mengenai Keresidenan Bangkahulu dan Palembang, in *Hukum* 1957 No. 3—4.
Meulen, J. D. van der, De Oorsprong van de Straf van Opsluiting, in *Mededelingen van het Documentatiebureau voor Overzees Recht,* Leiden 3de Jrg. 1953.
Meulen, J. D. van der, Artikel 161 bis Wetboek van Strafrecht, in *Mededelingen van het Documentatiebureau voor Overzees Recht,* Leiden 4de Jrg. 1954.
Mezger, E., A. Schönke & H. H. Jescheck, *Das ausländische Strafrecht der Gegenwart,* I (1955).
Moeljatno, *Perbuatan pidana dan pertanggungan djawab dalam Hukum Pidana,* pidato dies Djokjakarta 1955.
Mouton, M. W., *Oorlogsmisdrijven en het Internationale Recht,* diss. Leiden 1947.

Noyon, T. J., *Het Wetboek van Strafrecht* (6e dr. bewerkt door G. E. Langemeijer 1954).
Nulla poena sine lege, in *Tijdschrift voor Strafrecht,* Deel XLIV 1934.

Oppenheim, L., *International Law,* II (7th edition edited by H. Lauterpacht 1955).

Pompe, W. P. J., *De Persoon des Daders in het Strafrecht,* Inaug. Rede Utrecht 1928.
Pompe, W. P. J., *Handboek van het Nederlandse Strafrecht* (4de herz. dr. 1953).
Pompe, W. P. J., De Misdadige Mens, in *Tijdschrift voor Strafrecht,* Deel LXIII 1954.
Pompe, W. P. J., De Mens in het Strafrecht, in *Rechtsgeleerd magazijn Themis* 1957.
Prins, W. F., *Pengantar Ilmu Hukum Tata-Usaha Negara* (translated by R. Kosim Adisapoetra 1953).
Prodjodikoro, Wirjono, Tjatatan tentang tjara mendjalankan hukuman mati, postscript in *Hukum* 1959 No. 5—6.

Raliby, Osman, ed., *Documenta Historica* I (1953).
Röling, B. V. A., De Mens in het Recht, in *Scripta Academica Groningana VI,* 9de Interfacultaire Leergang 1954—1955.
Röling, B. V. A., De strafbaarheid van de rechtspersoon, in *Tijdschrift voor Strafrecht,* Deel LXVI 1957.
Röling, B. V. A., L'orientation moderne des notions d'auteur de l'infraction et de participation à l'infraction, in *Revue Internationale de Droit Pénal,* 27e année 1957.

Saito, Kinsaku, see Mezger, E.
Saleh, Roeslan, Perbuatan pidana dan dipidananja pembuat, in *Madjalah Hukum dan Masjarakat,* Tah. III No. 1 1958.
Sastranegara, R., *Hukum Tatanegara Indonesia.*
Schepper, J. M. J., *Het Vonnis in de P.N.I.-zaak* (1931).
Schiller, A. A., *The Formation of Federal Indonesia* (1955).
Schravendijk, H. J. van, *Buku peladjaran tentang Hukum Pidana Indonesia* (1956).
Seno Adji, Oemar, Kemerdekaan Pers di Indonesia, II in *Hukum* 1956 No. 1—2.

Seno Adji, Oemar, postscripts in *Hukum* 1956 No. 1—2 p. 103 ff, 1958 No. 3—4 p. 156 ff, 1959 No. 5—6 p. 45 ff.
Simons, D., *Leerboek van het Nederlandsche Strafrecht,* Deel I (6de dr. bijgew. door W. P. J. Pompe 1937).
Smit, C., *De Indonesische Quaestie* (1952).
Soenario, R., *Proses Jungschläger* (1956).
Soepomo, R., *Undang-undang Dasar Sementara Republik Indonesia* (1950).
Soepomo, R., *Kedudukan Hukum Adat dikemudian hari* (tjet. ke-2 1951).
De Straf van Opsluiting, in *Mededelingen van het Documentatiebureau voor Overzees Recht,* Leiden 2de Jrg. 1952.
Supomo, R., *Sistim Hukum di Indonesia (sebelum Perang Dunia II)* (tjet. ke-3 1957).

Territoriale Verscheidenheid in het Indonesisch Wetboekenstrafrecht, in *Mededelingen van het Documentatiebureau voor Overzees Recht,* Leiden 3de Jrg. 1953.
Tidow, A. R., *Der Schuldbegriff im englischen und nordamerikanischen Strafrecht,* Rechtsvergleichende Untersuchungen zur gesamten Strafrechtswissenschaft, neue Folge 5 (1952).
Traeger, L., Die zeitliche Herrschaft des Strafgesetzes, in *Vergleichende Darstellung des Deutschen und Ausländischen Strafrechts,* Allgemeiner Teil VI (1908).
Tresna, R., *Azas-azas Hukum Pidana* (1959).
Tussen Sawahs en Bergen, Het Leven van de Soldaat in de Tijgerbrigade (1948).

Utrecht, E., *Pengantar dalam Hukum Indonesia* (tjet. ke-4 1957).
Utrecht, E., *Hukum Pidana,* I (1958).
Utrecht, E., Beberapa tjatatan tentang suatu Hukum Pidana jang lebih kolektif, in *Padjadjaran,* Djilid I No. 1 1958.

Vervloet, L. Th., dan Mohamad Jusuf, *Pelanggaran Ekonomi di Indonesia, Economische Delicten in Indonesië* (1954).
Vinacke, Harold M., *Far Eastern Politics in the postwar period* (1956).
Vos, H. B., *Leerboek van Nederlands Strafrecht* (3de herz. dr. 1950).

Waard, R. de, De strafbaarheid van het feit naast de strafbaarheid van den dader, in *Tijdschrift voor Strafrecht,* Deel LIX 1950.
Wehl, David, *The Birth of Indonesia* (1948).
Woodman, Dorothy, *The Republic of Indonesia* (1955).

Yamin, Muhammad, *Proklamasi dan Konstitusi Republik Indonesia* (tjet. ke-2 1952).
Yearbook on Human Rights for 1949.

Zevenbergen, W., *Leerboek van het Nederlandsche Strafrecht* (1924).
Zorab, A. A., *De Japanse Bezetting van Indonesië en haar volkenrechtelijke zijde,* diss. Leiden 1954.

ABBREVIATIONS

B.N.R.I.S.	*Berita Negara Republik Indonesia Serikat.*
K.U.H.P.	*Kitab Undang-undang Hukum Pidana.*
L.N.	*Lembaran Negara.*
M.D.B.	*Mededelingen van het Documentatiebureau voor Overzees Recht, Leiden.*
S.	*Staatsblad.*
T.	*Indisch Tijdschrift van het Recht.*
T.L.N.	*Tambahan Lembaran Negara.*
W.v.S. I.	*Wetboek van Strafrecht voor Indonesië.*
W.v.S. N.I.	*Wetboek van Strafrecht voor Nederlandsch-Indië.*